Ritual
&
The Arts
In
Spiritual Discernment

Ritual & The Arts In Spiritual Discernment

Cover design: Chelle Cox

Printed in the United States of America: Lightning Print, LaVergne, TN

ISBN 0-9672959-0-4

This book is dedicated to
all who have journeyed with me
along the path of spiritual discernment,
especially the members of my religious community,
the Sisters of Charity, BVM,
my colleague, Charles M. Olsen,
and our network of associates at
WORSHIPFUL-WORK
Center for Transforming Religious Leadership.

CONTENTS

INTRODUCTION

Those of us living in the United States today experience the winds of God's Spirit blowing where they will, at unexpected times, and in unlikely places. Though we live in a country where there is much cultural shifting and political change, I sense that a great cosmological awareness is making swift progress. Even on a global scale there seems to be a deeper realization that the universe is infused and pervaded by a spiritual presence. Persons are yearning for a transformed consciousness about all of creation, for a right ordering of the communal spirit, mind, heart and will. I firmly believe that the incorporation of ritual and the arts into the age-old decision making practice of spiritual discernment assists and deepens a transformed consciousness.

The content of this book is keyed to the "Movements" necessary in a process of spiritual discernment. These Movements are described in detail in *Discerning God's Will Together: A Spiritual Practice for the Church* by my colleague at Worshipful-Work: Center for Transforming Religious Leadership, Dr. Charles M. Olsen, and co-author Danny E. Morris, formerly Director of Developing Ministries of The Upper Room in Nashville, Tennessee. This book is meant to assist a person who facilitates spiritual discernment, a discernmentarian (akin to a parliamentarian who facilitates parliamentary procedure), with suggestions for incorporating ritual and the arts into the Movements of spiritual discernment.

A process of spiritual discernment invites persons into God-discovery and self-discovery. Spiritual discernment invites communal sharing of assumptions about God, about ourselves, and about the process itself. Spiritual discernment challenges us to an in-depth exploration of the ramifications of a decision. The looked for outcome is a decision that will bring about God's yearning or will for us.

The Hebrew scriptures includes many stories of persons who searched in earnest for God's will or yearning. Among them was Moses, who reminded the Israelites of their great failures during the desert years, and warned them to be wary of temptations in the future. To name a few others, Eijah, Samuel, Jeremiah, Jacob also were persons captivated by God. They had a transforming experience in knowing God. They made every effort to see and hear from God's perspective, often coming to identify with God's yearning for justice and for the poor in their very midst.

The New Testament is also rich in examples of spiritual discernment. It is the words of the indigent woman, Mary, in her magnificat, which have inspired change in individuals who have pondered those words, including the establishment of liberation movements in Latin America. Peter, who loved Jesus and believed him to be the Christ, at first wanted a Christ conformed to his own attachments, rather than the suffering Messiah. Individual and communal practicing of spiritual discernment, deep centering in the search for God's yearning, is capable of bringing about such transformation.

In the Christian Scriptures we find Paul numbering among the important gifts of God's Spirit that of discernment (1 Corinthians 12: 10). Paul's letters enumerate upon three relationships that are possible between a Christian community and the Spirit of God: 1) the absence of the Spirit, as in Galatians 5:19-21; 2); the presence of the Spirit, as in 1 Corinthians 12:3; and 3) the habitual direction by the Spirit of God, as in Galatians 5:25-26. Paul seems to strongly suggest that the practice of spiritual discernment enables one to participate in a progression from absence of light, very much like the movements of conversion, to life in God's Spirit.

Walter Brueggemann, in his book *Gathering the Church in the Spirit, Reflections on Exile and the Inscrutable Wind of God*, tells us that "all through the life and history of the church, God's spirit has come into the world to keep the people of God unsettled, open, on the move, and in obedient mission in fresh ways" (pg. 9). So, the stories we hear and tell provide a framework of symbols for making sense out of what is going on within us and around us. The facts we relate and the insights gained in a process of spiritual discernment, often take us from an absence of light through the tension of grappling with options, into the realm of mystery, and into life in God's Spirit. This journey helps us to articulate our values, our hopes and dreams, and celebrate, in ritual and through the arts, our hungers for "something more." These stories give significance to our particular life experiences that, for better or for worse, have been prompted by events or persons in our lives. They reveal elements of harmony and discord, as well as presence and absence of light and life.

Perusing the contents of this book may be for you an experience like that of moving through a spiritual labyrinth. I make no apologies for this because there are many possible ways of incorporating ritual and the arts into spiritual discernment. This book is meant to lead you down some of those paths. Of course, there are still unexplored paths.

As a facilitator of spiritual discernment, you are invited to:

- ponder the befriending Spirit of God as you peruse the contents of this book;
- find the holy in the wisdom of various cultures and spiritualities described here, and from others upon which you will draw;
- be mindful of the interconnectedness and spiritual energy that joins all living things;
- increasingly trust your own intuition, imagination and resources as well as those of the persons with whom you will interact in a process of spiritual discernment.

It is my hope that the time you spend in preparation for serving as a discernmentarian will result in excitement about being involved in the workings of God's Spirit. And, it is my hope that you will personally come to know the heart, the center, the *being* and *doing* of spiritual discernment, and some rituals and artistic possibilities for coming to this place. I invite you to choose ideas that will be helpful to you in your ministry, and I encourage you to invite others to bring their ideas and artistic gifts into the process. It is to this end that I offer you my reflections in this book.

Chapter One

Ritual
In Spiritual Discernment

Who *does* ritual? A liturgist? A presider? A preacher or homilist? A choir? The musicians? All of these and more. The gathered assembly! One description of ritual (or liturgy) is this: "Each church gathers regularly to praise and thank God, to remember and make present God's great deeds, to offer common prayer, to realize and celebrate the kingdom of peace and justice."[1]

Ritual (from "ritis" - custom) is, however, not limited to a specific place and time on Sunday mornings. Praising God in song and silence, listening to, pondering and remembering God's great deeds throughout time, blessing each other, interceding for the many needs of our world, exchanging greetings of peace -- all these need to coexist with daily lives that praise, listen, ponder and remember, bless, intercede and greet -- day by day and year by year.

It is commonplace to think of ritual as a sequence of behavior that is orderly, regular in occurrence, occupying the mind and emotions and having some general social affect. To a structuralist such as John McManus, ritual behavior is neurobiologically "wired in" throughout the entire animate universe. It is expressed in varied ranges from a primitive "molecular" organization to those complex systems of cognition and social relationships of which a string quartet performance is an example.[2] It appears to me that this neurobiological approach gives notice that ritual is an unexceptional aspect of much of human behavior.

The concept of ritual as experiential glue that holds society together seems to more congenially describe ritual as I am interpreting it in this book. Traditional rituals need not be fixed and stagnant but can

---

[1] Mary Ann Simcoe, ed. The Liturgy Documents. "Environment and Art in Catholic Worship", Chicago, IL: Liturgy Training Publications, 1978, p 270.

[2] John McManus, Eugene d'Aquili, Charles Laughlin, Tom Burns, eds. The Spectrum of Ritual: A Bioenic Structural Analysis. New York, NY: Columbia University Press, 1979, p 212.

1

become new with reinterpretation. As human beings we are composed of mind, body and spirit. So we can involve our whole selves in personal and communal rituals. We are free to use colors, words and symbols to express our group identity or ethos. In meaningful rituals we are not spectators, but responsive participants. We are all the celebrants of ritual. During meaningful rituals, we open ourselves to the mystery, wonder and awe of life; our senses are awakened and attuned to the God who graces our gatherings.

To confine God's Spirit to words alone is to rob ourselves of visual, tangible and symbolic vehicles of grace in spiritual discernment. To deal with words alone is to tear down or ignore an available bridge between ourselves and the Spirit of God.

Divergent theological views and pastoral practices characterized the Reformation period of the Sixteenth Century. Protestants generally preferred few embellishments for their rituals, while Roman Catholics embraced visual displays of the baroque. The reformers focused on congregational song, while Roman Catholic ritual sought a more restrained style of Latin polyphony. In general, Protestant churches rejected the emphasis on the visual and concentrated on the auditory. Roman Catholic churches made few concessions to the members of the assembly in its reforms, reducing the assembly to silent spectators.

Edward Foley, in his book, *From Age To Age*, writes that the various developments during that time in church history "fall into four categories: elaboration, elimination, substitution and invention."[3] Let me give an example of each category: 1) Elaboration: vessels were great works of art that sometime previously graced the tables of the wealthy; 2) Elimination: many reformation churches purged their images (iconoclasm) and vessels; 3) Substitution: a simplified Eucharist used domestic vessels, reminiscent of the early church; 4) Invention: Foley writes that the use of individual cups for communion "popularized scientific theory and pastoral convenience above the ancient symbol of one cup for the one community of faith."[4]

I am advocating in spiritual discernment a reformed use of ritual and the arts which is not to be considered extraneous. My experience with, and practice of, spiritual discernment tells me that we really do

---

[3] Edward Foley. From Age To Age. Chicago, IL: Liturgy Training Publications, 1991, p 136.

[4] Ibid, p 137.

2

need more than words to assist us in grasping the intimate relatedness of our humanity and God's transcendence.

A prayerful process of discernment will incorporate meaningful rituals into its very core. Rituals may alternate between persons and groups of persons, between sound and silence, speech and song, movement and stillness, proclamation and reflection. The use of rituals or art forms should never interrupt a discernment process. Properly used, rituals serve to enhance, support and illumine the process.

A discernmentarian, who is also the group's liturgist -- one who takes initiative in drawing the group into awareness of God's presence during their time together -- should prepare some rituals in advance, but should also allow room for others to arise within the process. Very meaningful rituals are occasionally initiated by group members who have no prior knowledge of, or experience with, spiritual discernment in a group context.

As I prepare to assume the ministry of discernmentarian, I find it most helpful to reflect on the "Elements of Ritual" which Gabe Huck, in his book *How Can I Keep From Singing*, articulates so well. They are these: There is a place, a room. There are things. There are movements, gestures, postures. There are words. There is time itself. Rituals are the deeds of people. Rituals are done by heart.[5]

♦ **"There is a place, a room."**

The process of evoking "a place" for spiritual discernment, a space for God's Spirit to breathe within the group, is a key component of the process. The visual and acoustical specialness of a place, a room, can either distance people from a sense of God's presence or awaken in them a sense of divine immediacy.

Do you have a choice of place, e.g., a retreat center, a conference room? In what place, with definite or indefinite boundaries, will you gather for spiritual discernment? What does the space look like? How can it be made a gracious and inviting place, a space for worship and work, a place comfortable for the number of people who will gather there? Will the seating enable every participant to make eye contact with everyone in the group? Is the lighting appropriate and easy on the eyes?

---

[5] Gabe Huck. How Can I Keep From Singing? Thoughts About Liturgy For Musicians. Chicago, IL: Liturgy Training Publications, 1989.

In my experience, the most common gathering space for spiritual discernment is indoors, living rooms or chapel spaces. Sometimes church halls or basement rooms are used. The structure of these rooms may require great creativity on the part of a discernmentarian to convert them into comfortable, more intimate spaces. A certain flexibility or move-ability should be considered even for essential furnishings. Care should be taken to choose or arrange a place of simple beauty. And, it is important that those less physically able can participate without unnecessary strain or burden.

Good weather, however, could inspire enthusiasm for meeting in a quiet park or in a garden, by the seashore, or on a mountain nature trail. The impact of such awesome beauty could trigger a realization during spiritual discernment that one's ideas about the matter of discernment are altogether too narrow. St. Paul writes about being anointed by the Holy Spirit, which could be a metaphor for an experience of having one's heart and mind suddenly or gradually understand in a moment of appreciation for a natural wonder.

When meeting indoors, I suggest that the group meet in the same space each time it gathers. I once dealt with gathering in a different home for each discernment session. "Turf" ownership, among other things, began to interfere with the group's abilities to achieve even small steps toward consensus. Persons didn't want to offend someone who had shown such great hospitality (which then led to one-ups man-or woman-ship!). Choosing a neutral space really does make a difference in the way participants can enter and go deeper into a process of spiritual discernment.

◆   **"There are things."**

As humans we often take "things" for granted. While we may not always concern ourselves with such elements as forms, textures and colors, we are born into worlds of symbolic meaning. At the heart of our cultured way of life are symbols that embody the particular spirit of a people. The meanings of our varied cultures are transmitted by their symbols. The death of Princess Diana called to the world's attention the British culture, with speculations and commentaries about its inherent flaws. We can take the symbols of our cultures so for granted that they are called to our explicit attention only if something goes wrong.

We are humans rooted in this earth and yet restless here, searching for a sense of our connectedness. The appropriate use of symbols in spiritual discernment will connect not only our heads, but our hearts. The experience of mystery which spiritual discernment offers is found in its God-centeredness. This involves a certain beneficial tension with the demands of an environment that invites contemplation, or seeing beyond a thing into the holy. A simple and attractive beauty in everything that is used is the most effective invitation into this kind of experience. Things used in spiritual discernment should have more than quality; they should have a kind of transparency, so that we see and experience both the work of art and something beyond it. Their vitality will depend upon the connection we are able to make between everyday life and the community's rituals. Through the use of appropriate, beautiful and simple things, the meanings of ordinary life become enlarged to the point of coming more clearly into focus. This book is devoted to the task of presenting ideas that flow out of the dynamic point of view that symbols magnify life's day-to-day meanings.

Let me further explain the terminology used here. Words that are popularly used in very similar ways can have different connotations. The difference between sign and symbol is one example.

A sign is a matter of fact, something general, something anyone can relate to, even across language barriers. A stop sign is something very general; it is impersonal, it signifies a warning, and it issues a command. A symbol on the other hand, is deeply personal. A symbol represents some other reality; it goes deeper than a sign. This is because a symbol draws upon elusive meaning that is at home in our memories and imaginations. We linger in memory and imagination over a symbol, such as a letter of special recognition or a beloved photograph. A sign gives us all there is to be said or done in a given situation. In the use of symbols, we contribute at least half the meaning and action.

A discernmentarian should invite an awareness and a celebration of personal and communal symbols in such a way that each participant's symbols of a special insight, a wondrous moment, or an experience of pain will not seem to be too precious or intimate to be shared. A discernmentarian needs to foster the capacity to connect traditional and biblical symbols with personal symbols.

The prayerful rhythm of the church year, a predictable pattern of decisive events in our faith history, provides many "things" or symbols that are wonderfully familiar, yet they can help us transcend the ordinary, earthly elements that they are: seeds, songs, bread, wine, water, oil, fire... For example, think about the season of Advent. The days are shorter and the nights long. During this liturgical season, we, like the fields, lie fallow and waiting. All that is becoming is hidden from our sight. We long for the return of the sun and the birth of the Word made flesh. – People's hearts usually resonate with seasonal symbols, if not always rational theology.

If you are gathering indoors, what in the room needs to be removed, covered or rearranged? What would you add, e.g., hymnbooks? How might you create a centering focus, e.g., candle, Bible, a cloth the color of the liturgical season? I suggest that *less is more*. I also believe that symbols used in spiritual discernment should, if at all possible, be real and not artificial, e.g., not plastic, but real flowers. They should reflect the size, means, and need of the gathered community. In other words, they should not be set apart from the assembly whose needs they are meant to serve.

If you are gathering outdoors, what things are essential for prayerful reflection in addition to the bounty of nature? Would a wind chime, streamers, a balloon, pinwheel, kite or a candle provide a simple centering focus for prayer? Should there be one Bible or should everyone bring his/her own? Would seating pads and writing tablets facilitate your time together?

The most important aspect to remember is that things used in spiritual discernment should nurture, not detract, from the group's prayerful work.

♦   **"There are movements, gestures, postures."**

How will people enter the room or the space? Is the entrance conducive to loud noise or to the quieting of one's inner thoughts or anxieties? Imagine the participants coming through a labyrinth. They may have had a hard day at the office or have been stressed by a situation at home. Will the entrance space cause them to rush in or to slow down their pace? Can it be made more welcoming by the addition of quiet colors such as blue, burgundy or cream, with greenery, or with soft music? Discernmentarians certainly can borrow ideas from interior designers who use colors to effectively reduce persons' anxieties during

6

appointments with professional health or social services.

What actions can you plan for ahead of time that will involve the whole group, e.g., standing and encircling a candle for prayer, closing eyes for a silent or guided meditation, lighting a candle, passing a lit candle around the group while a blessing is offered for the person holding the candle, blessing water, breaking bread, clasping hands, planting seeds, swaying to the rhythm of a hymn, etc. Movements, gestures and postures, if they genuinely add a richness to our prayer, engage our whole persons. When they do this, they are not ostentatious, theatrical or purely entertaining. They are very much an integral part of the whole experience. They are akin to prayerful play, wherein persons extend themselves into a deeper experience of God's Spirit alive within the community. Spontaneous movements, gestures and postures, those completely unplanned, may also cause deep engagement in the group's prayer or conversation.

One of my most profound experiences in the use of gestures during a process of spiritual discernment happened when a hearing impaired person spontaneously signed the Lord's Prayer as the rest of us voiced it. Everyone was struck by the power of the gestures as well as the grace of the hand movements. This prayer came to be very significant for our group, and was done very much by heart each time we gathered.

The practice of "laying on of hands" is an action or gesture that expresses the community's role in encouraging, fostering, discerning and receiving the Spirit's gifts. This hand gesture done on the head, the shoulders or arms, can be done with a person/s standing, kneeling, sitting or even lying down. It has abundant use outside of sacramental actions, i.e., reconciliation, anointing of the sick. Joined with the invocation of Christ's name and memory, this gesture has the power to be a transforming experience for those so blessed.

Some movements and gestures take on monumental significance when done by a large congregation. But there is nothing to prevent a smaller group commemorating a significant Biblical/liturgical event. A song of praise could be sung as the group moves around an indoor or outdoor space waving palm branches in commemoration of the Palm Sunday drama.

The space in which the group will meet for spiritual discernment can be blessed with a series of gestures and movements. When the building which houses our ministry was dedicated in 1995, we involved those present in a blessing of the space. Tree branches were brought to the dedication and placed in the center of the room alongside a large, empty bowl. In the course of the celebration, water from pottery pitchers was poured into the large bowl, blessed, and then the branches were dipped in the water. Participants scattered within and outside the building, blessing every nook and cranny.

While gestures, postures and movements have always been part of our liturgies, dance movement is a more recent development rooted in the desire to include cultural elements that validly express our faith. Clement of Alexandria, in the Second Century, spoke of prayer as involving hands and feet. Throughout most of the Nineteenth Century, the Shakers made dance an important part of their worship. Native American and African American peoples intuit that drumming and dancing are very natural ways to worship.

A discerning community in need of fresh movements, gestures and postures need only learn to look for them in the wedding of their own cultures with Biblical stories of ministry, and in their experience of God's Spirit at work in their community and in the world. Our prayer, our discerning, is rooted in memory. In other words, it springs from remembering God's gracious actions in Christ, and from the accompanying recognition of that gracious love still at work in the world. Much of Christianity today is in a stage of recovery of early practices and concepts.

Take note of the cultures represented in the members of the discernment group. What movements, gestures and postures could they bring to the experience of spiritual discernment? Harvest the prayerful energy of these persons, their creation spirituality, their ability to produce beauty in various forms. Encourage these expressions and invite the group to participate in them to the degree in which they are comfortable. Remember that they should not be extraneous to the experience of the group, but be integral to the prayerful gathering.

♦　　**"There are words."**

Words provide a vital link between inner experience and outward clarification of that experience. Human relations depend upon words and how they are used. The timing, choice and tone of words can often make the difference between conflict or enjoyment in human interactions.

We need words. We are people fashioned by the words of our nourishing God. We are born out of covenants and promises that have been expressed in words for thousands of years. Our memories burn with words carved on stone tablets and written on scrolls.

In spiritual discernment, we need words that are connected to our hearts. We need words that have potential for life, that enable us to move toward understanding each other at a deeper level. We needs words that reveal God's presence, not hide it. We need words that illumine, not which provide for keeping secrets. For Jesus, it was not enough for his followers to simply hear the Word, agree with it and then live as they had before receiving it. Jesus was not after agreement. He was after personal change and radical commitment to the Word.

In spiritual discernment, we need to use words not so much to describe data, but to break through the surface to the real truth. We use words to give honest expression to the word of God within us.

While our words cannot contain or confine God, they can, like the world itself, be icons, avenues of approach, numinous presences, ways of touching without totally grasping or seizing.

What words will you prepare ahead of time? What words will be sung? What words will you use to invite storytelling, prayers of intercession, thanksgiving, forgiveness or praise?

Inviting the discerners to name their images of God in a prayerful litany can provide the group with new, rich images that may foster further exploration personally, or in the group. I usually suggest a simple response to affirm each naming, e.g., "You are with us here."

Are there words that need to be printed for the participants, or displayed in the room where you are gathered? Marshall McLuhan once observed that print is the technology of individualism. An insightful discernmentarian will guard against this becoming true! She/he will have only what "print" needs to be available for each participant.

Incorporating Lectio Divina, a prayerful reading of scripture in spiritual discernment engages the whole person: mind, heart and spirit. Lectio Divina is not a technique, but a process. St. John of the Cross paraphrased a verse from Luke 11:9 to explain Lectio Divina to his contemporaries. This serves well as an outline of the process: "Seek in reading (lectio) and you will find in meditation (meditatio); knock in prayer (oratio) and it will be opened to you in contemplation (contemplatio)." [6]

Dom Marmion, a French Benedictine monk, gives us another guide: "We read (lectio) under the eye of God (meditatio) until the heart is touched (oratio) and leaps to flame (contemplatio)." [7] The key to meditation and contemplation is the silence between the words. Silence is our guide into the mystery in spiritual discernment.

Yes, there is joy in hearing sounds. And yes, there is joy in their absence. Yes, there are heartfelt prayers using words, and yes, there are many prayers for which we can find no words. Spiritual discernment involves a balance between spoken words and silence.

T. S. Eliot, in his magnificent poem *Ash Wednesday*, says, "Is there enough silence for the Word to be heard?"[8] Is there enough silence in ourselves for God's presence to be felt? Note the importance of words, strong enough to bear the weight of repetition, mystery and reverence in the poem *Words*, by Ann Sexton:

> *"Be careful of words,*
> *even the miraculous ones.*
> *For the miraculous we do our best.*
> *Sometimes they swarm like insects*
> *and leave not a sting but a kiss.*
> *They can be as good as fingers.*
> *They can be as trusty as the rock*
> *you stick your bottom on.*
> *But they can be both daisies and bruises.*
>
> *Yet I am in love with words.*
> *They are doves falling out of the ceiling.*
> *They are six holy oranges sitting in my lap.*
> *They are the trees, the legs of summer,*
> *and the sun, its passionate face.*
> *Yet often they fail me.*

---

[6] Thelma Hall. Too Deep For Words, Rediscovering Lectio Divina. Mahwah, NJ: Paulist Press, 1988 p 28.

[7] Ibid., p 44.

[8] T.S. Eliot. Ash Wednesday. New York, NY: Harcourt Brace & Co., 1934, p 55.

I have so much I want to say,
so many stories, images, proverbs, etc.
But the words aren't good enough,
the wrong ones kiss me.
Sometimes I fly like an eagle
but with the wings of a wren.

But I try to take care
and be gentle to them.
Words and eggs must be handled with care.
Once broken they are impossible
things to repair."[9]

♦   **"There is time itself."**

After a few years of using one, I still find it hard to get used to my digital alarm clock. This clock shows me only the present hour and minute, but not the present time in relationship to the whole circle of day and night. With my previous, now old-fashioned alarm clock, time was obviously cyclic. I could look forward and backwards. It helped me reflect on the past hours and anticipate future times.

Those of us with a Judeo-Christian heritage traditionally celebrate past and future times, a cycle of festivals. Year after church year, we are given a sense of belonging to this faith continuum by celebrating the church years and their liturgical seasons. This prayerful rhythm of the church year provides an abundance of resources for each gathering of the assembly, as the lectionary contains Scripture passages for each day and for the Sunday celebrations.

As pastoral administrator of a parish and its mission church in the Diocese of Great Falls-Billings, Montana in the mid-1980's, I had the opportunity to facilitate what came to be the eventual closing of a mission church. Of course when the Bishop presented this opportunity to me, I didn't relish the thought of it. A pastor does not usually endear oneself to a congregation by attempting such an action!

---

[9] Ann Sexton "Words," The Awful Towing Toward God. Boston, MA: Houghton Mifflin Co., 1975, p 71.

11

As someone who did not relish being a new pastoral presence with such a goal in mind, I asked the Bishop to give me at least three years to assess the situation and to accomplish, in some collaborative way, that almost certain outcome. As interested as I was in assuming my new ministry, the thought of figuring out how to bring closure to a long-standing parish mission church gave me much food for thought and prayer!

During the initial months of driving the seventy miles roundtrip to preside at worship every Saturday night, I gradually uncovered many facts of life about this mission church family. I gathered many statistics and antidotes, but my most telling discovery was that "church" meant a building of convenience.

I won't tell the whole story here, but let it suffice for me to say that not having other case studies to read on the closing of parishes in the 1980's (the 1990's are providing more than enough examples of how *not* to close parishes), and after assessing the situation for two years, I came up with the idea of using the liturgical calendar as the focus for a process of facing the reality of the future of this mission church. From Advent of 1986 through Lent of 1987, I developed a process that would lead toward an eventual group decision.

The process literally evolved day by day and week by week. It involved reflections on the birth of the community and some years of stability. Because our Christian lives are centered in the mystery of dying and rising to new life in Jesus Christ, I remember asking questions such as: "Are we being fed by the stories of life, by bread, wine, conversation, outreach to others and interactions with neighboring communities?" "Do I/we savor our community and foster it? In what ways?" "What limitations do we experience in living out our baptismal call in this community?"

By winter of 1987, the time for beginning our lenten journey, the congregation came to name, with anger, the decline of their church. There just was no future for this small church as a worshipping community. I remember a parishioner saying to me, "You're not to blame for this situation. We've known this decision was coming." This public comment and others began the process of letting go of the past and taking hold of the present.

Did I help the obvious decision to be made? I believe so. But I couldn't stop there. We needed to rise to some new form of life. The active parishioners needed to be able to call some worship space their new home.

The last service at the church was on Good Friday. Following the prescribed ritual and a period of silence (with many tears), we ritualized with sacred movements and verbal prayers the removal of the tabernacle, the crucifix, the altar, the altar stone, the lectern and the cross which hung on the outside of the building. The altar was dismantled and buried and the altar stone taken to the "mother church" which I also served. Before the ritual concluded, I invited each person present to name the parish they would be welcomed into on Easter Sunday.

This is indeed a sacred story. It's a story of anger, denial, grieving, closure, and eventual re-birth of this small community into becoming part of two existing faith communities. God's Word, opened and broken and shared in spiritual discernment over a long period of time --God's own time--worked wonders we could not have accomplished within another manner of meeting together.

When the group gathers for spiritual discernment, will you gather in daytime or in the evening? What time, or season of the year, is it?

It can be very appropriate for a discernmentarian to anticipate the Sunday celebration by choosing a particular text for reflection, especially if its usage has apparent value for the immediate conversation at hand. The following Sunday celebration will then provide the group with yet another opportunity to hear God's Word, reflect on it, and let it go deeper into the heart and mind of the group.

For centuries, spiritual writers have urged us to come at life reflectively. They have taught us differing ways of punctuating our days and our nights with points of rest wherein we romance the Divine, wherein we find God. The daily Office, or Liturgy of the Hours, provides a rhythm of prayer for personal and group use around the clock. Each hour of prayer has certain characteristic themes. In evening, the descent of darkness hints of death, but in the paradox of paschal time, death is the moment of birth. Evening prayer really marks the beginning rather than the end of the liturgical day. The traditional texts for evening invite us to look back to give thanks for the day behind us, and forward to welcome the promised light or morning. Additional night and day hours round out the cycle of daily prayer.

The Liturgy of the Hours follows this cyclic pattern:

- *Compline* or evening prayer, a time for resting in God after

13

reflection on the day, when thanksgivings are offered and confessions are made;

- *Matins* or night prayer, a time of trusting in God as we lose control of our physical bodies and through meditation and dreaming, let our whole being worship God;
- *Lauds* at daybreak, when we hope in God's presence and promise;
- *Prime*, shortly thereafter, during which we reflect on our call to faithful discipleship;
- *Terce*, or mid-morning prayer, with continued expectation of sharing in the work of God's creation that day;
- *Sext*, prayer at mid-day, around noon, when we call ourselves to practice seeing Christ in others in the midst of our work, ministry and activities; and
- *None*, our mid-afternoon prayer that gives voice to the events of the day and God's presence in them.
- *Vespers*, prayer at the end of our working day, a time for offering thanks for events of the day and graces received.

In the Liturgy of the Hours, with only a few exceptions, the psalms follow a cyclic pattern of four weeks with a seasonal antiphon prayed before and after each psalm. Some books suggest psalms to be sung as well as music to include which speaks to the particular time of prayer, e.g., "Morning Has Broken" or "Day Is Done." The psalm and antiphon for each part of the day/night is followed by a reading from Scripture. There is time set aside for intercessory prayers. Canticles are prayed during morning and evening prayer. A closing prayer always concludes a particular Liturgy of the Hours.

It is good for discernmentarians to share this available rhythm of prayer for personal or communal discernment. To assist persons in using this forms of prayer which evolved during the time of monasticism, there are many available copies of the Liturgy of the Hours in paperback, as well as leather bound books. A good and inexpensive publishing resource is the Carmelite Monastery, 2500 Cold Spring Road, Indianapolis, IN 46222.

Another resource for a discernmentarian is *The Liturgy of the Hours*, by Dominic F. Scotto. His book contains a historical survey, examines documents on the reform of the Liturgy of the Hours, and explores pastoral considerations surrounding their implementation.

14

Now, given that most of us are not monastics with the habit of rising for prayer throughout the night, how can a discernmentarian take the best of this tradition and suggest incorporation of the Liturgy of the Hours into personal and communal spiritual discernment? Let me ask some leading questions, then you can decide for yourself.

Will you be gathering after the day's work? Could you begin the gathering with Vespers, prayer at the end of the working day, and close the gathering with Compline, or Evening Prayer?

Could you invite the group to covenant with each other to pray Lauds at daybreak for the intention of the group between meeting times, every day or a certain number of days per week?

Will the group be gathering over a whole day's time? Mid-morning, mid-day, mid-afternoon prayer could be prayed in solitude or with the group, or varied as best befits the desires of the participants.

When a group is together, what specific times can be designated for silence? Times of silence serve to focus our energies, calm our thoughts, relax our bodies, and help us center ourselves in God's indwelling Spirit. Perhaps you may wish to invite two to five minutes of silence to be shared by the whole group. At another time, the developing process may call for fifteen or even thirty minutes of silence spent in stillness or in journaling. An intuitive discernmentarian will sense when such time should be taken.

Does the time you are structuring for the gathering seem adequate for a prayerful, non-rushed agenda? Is it too short? Is it too long? One only can be sure by testing, but a good rule of thumb is to allow for a minimum of two to three hours for an initial gathering of the group. My suggestion is to allow at least this much time for successive gatherings.

♦   **"Rituals are the deeds of people."**

How can you best engage everyone in the group in meaningful rituals? There is no audience in spiritual discernment. The process belongs to everyone involved in it. The journey into spiritual discernment is meant to be one of building community, so the discernmentarian may wish to lead the participants in a dialogue about group development theory using language that addresses the formation of

15

community in the context of baptismal call. Let me explain.

A healthy spiritual discernment group should experience moving through these particular stages of group development: 1) the "Polite" stage, where members are just getting acquainted and testing their first impressions of each other, to 2) the "Why Are We Here?" stage, when the purpose of the group is defined after conversation and clarification time, to 3) the "Bid for Power" stage, wherein group members make efforts to influence the thinking of the group and conflicts arise, to 4) the "Constructive" stage, where members have formed an identity and there is acceptance of each other's differing attitudes and values, onto 5) the "Esprit" stage, where the trust level is very high, resulting in good group morale and the personal satisfaction of members.[10]

Your role as discernmentarian throughout the process and through these stages should also be discussed with the group. Discernmentarians are usually wise enough to know that the process doesn't depend upon their expertise; they trust God more than themselves. But the group needs to hear you say this. The group should know right up front that you will not be making a decision for them, but be guiding them in a decision making process. They should know that you are familiar with the struggle of spiritual journeying and you will be supportive of their quest.

Now we know that in every spiritual discernment group the above named progression won't entirely be the case. But, in spiritual discernment, participants should sincerely attempt to move successfully through these stages of group development as an act of living out their baptism. Through baptism we have been immersed in the waters of divine life, called into continual conversion. The waters of baptism strengthen us for life in a world of ambiguity, and the waters challenge us to live lives of holiness: respecting differences among ourselves, and serving one another. It is out of our baptismal call then, that participants in spiritual discernment strive to bring their very best selves into the process, with assurance that the process is all about spirituality in Christ and about the giftedness of God's grace through the Spirit.

Since the church is united by baptism, how in word and deed is this going to be expressed? Well, as discernmentarian, it is initially your role to be *the* minister of hospitality. However, as the group progresses

---

[10] Ellen Morseth. Call To Leadership: Transforming the Local Church. Kansas City, MO: Sheed & Ward, 1993. p 41.

through the movements of spiritual discernment and through the stages of group development, as the group "jells", every member of the group will be joining you in building up the community.

♦   **"Rituals are done by heart."**

When we engage in Sunday worship, unless we are in an unfamiliar setting or context, most everyone knows the order of the service. We understand the movements and flow. Words and tunes are familiar, though they change with the seasons or for special days. We can even anticipate some movements. Many forms of prayer and symbolic expression combine to form an experience of prayer.

Doing "by heart" is when we see through a ritual in a double sense. In one sense we see "by way of" the environment, with its symbols, participants, its elements of music and silence, etc., as stimulators of religious experience. In another sense we see "beyond" this material reality, or beyond visible expression. In this second sense, the ritual evokes the presence of God revealed at a depth we cannot easily describe. It is out of this "heart" perception that we participate in ritual, not simply from rote memory (actions or words) but from our inner connectedness, or our depth.

In our contemporary Western culture, *head* and *heart* describe separate spheres. *Head* signifies our rational and analytic functions while *heart* refers to our feelings. But to comprehend the richness of *heart* in ritual, we need to understand its meaning in the Judeo-Christian tradition. In Jewish tradition, the heart is the center of the whole person, the core of personal character, including thought, emotion, intuition, will and imagination. Thoughts both good and evil arise from the heart, as well as motives and desires. When the heart is turned toward God, it is filled with grace and truth. When the heart turns away from God, it dwells in delusion. Prayerful rituals, then, those done "by heart" have us responding to God with our entire beings. We are moved both in our feelings and in our commitment to a deep relationship with God and all of God's creation.

"In African-American culture the emotional is not the opposite of the spiritual, nor is there any separation between the emotional and the

intellectual. Both the mind and the heart are needed to grasp the truth."[11]
So, "done by heart" is free and spontaneous. It overcomes the matter-of-
fact, immediate or concrete aspects of our rituals. It involves a readiness
to succumb to subtle feelings and attitudes which are awakened by God's
Spirit when the experience of ritual speaks directly to our souls, to the
conscious and subconscious layers of our minds, and certainly to our
hearts.

In his book, *Transforming Church Boards into Communities of
Spiritual Leaders*, my colleague, Dr. Charles M. Olsen illustrates some
transforming "practices" which we believe are integral not only to the
model of "worshipful-work" but to a process of spiritual discernment
and the ritual possibilities that lie within it. These practices do not stand
in isolation from each other, nor are they necessarily practiced in a
sequential order. These interlocking and interactive practices are:

- *the practice of History Giving or Storytelling (Coming from
  Somewhere).*
  Personal faith stories and stories of the ministry or group are
  told. "Corporate memory " is formed. Congregations,
  church boards and councils which have a sense of story or
  journey and an awareness that God is a player with a role in
  the story, tend to be congregations of vital faith.

- *the practice of Biblical and Theological Reflection
  (Distilling Wisdom).*
  Congregations, church boards and councils that engage in
  weaving their stories with Biblical stories and theological
  reflection, access faith traditions and see their own story in
  significant relationship to these traditions. They distill the
  wisdom by asking: What are the meanings, values, beliefs,
  purpose and mission?

- *the practice of Visioning the Future (Going Somewhere).*
  "Vision is the gift of divine eyes for seeing the future as it

---

[11] Jamie Phelps, "Black Spirituality", <u>Spiritual Traditions for the Contemporary
Church,</u> ed. Robin Mass and Gabriel O'Donnell. Nashville, TN: Abingdon
Press, 1990, p 342.

18

could be."[12] The distilled wisdom is projected into a future
setting.

- *the practice of Prayerful Discernment (Seeing with Spiritual
  Eyes).*
  "Discernment is the gift of seeing things as they are in the
  here and now. ... The issue in discernment becomes "What
  is God's will and call?"[13]

These practices--how we can incorporate Storytelling, Biblical
and Theological Reflection and Visioning the Future--will be alluded to
as we further discuss possibilities for their incorporation into the process
of Spiritual Discernment in this book.

So, ritual is what we humans do over and over, not by rote or
merely by memory, but " by heart." Rituals for celebrating birthdays,
weddings and anniversaries often retain certain common elements, but
they are enacted, with variations, year after year. So, too, as a group
enters more and more deeply into the practice of spiritual discernment,
the heart of the group will surface. This is the way it is with ritual. It is
then that the tools of human expression -- words, sounds, gestures,
objects, order, rhythm, practices -- will equip and begin to embody the
group's life and prayer.

And so it is then, that ritual assists persons in the process of
spiritual discernment. We have all of these elements upon which to
draw, and our creativity as discernmentarians is limited only by our
imaginations.

---

[12] Charles M. Olsen, <u>Transforming Church Boards into Communities of
Spiritual Leaders</u>. Washington, D.C.: The Alban Institute, 1995, p 106.
[13] Ibid

Chapter Two

ᏋᏂᏋ *Arts*
In Spiritual Discernment

"A person should hear a little music, read a little poetry, and see a fine picture every day in order that worldly cares may not obliterate the sense of the beautiful which God has implanted in the human soul."[14]

Have you ever felt as I have -- refreshed and energized, with a renewed sense of life -- after visiting an art museum, or turning on the radio and hearing one of your favorite musical compositions, or Maya Angelou read her poem "On the Pulse of Morning?" Then you may well imagine that incorporating the arts into a process of spiritual discernment will refresh and energize it.

In this Chapter, I am going to make some general comments about the using the arts in spiritual discernment, both Fine Art--art requiring highly developed techniques and skills and produced or intended chiefly for beauty rather than utility, e.g., sculpture and mosaics, and art that is produced by ordinary folks--the production of sounds, colors, forms, movements or other elements in ways that also affect the aesthetic sense, e.g., a weaver's art or the art of storytelling.

The following Chapters will provide some practical suggestions for incorporating ritual and the arts (both observing art and creating art) into the ten specific Movements of spiritual discernment.

POETRY

Poetry, certainly those poems contained in this book and others, serve to enhance a process of spiritual discernment. Poetry can be used in part, or in whole, for silent contemplation, or for recitation by individuals and/or a group in a variety of ways. Poetry can be used, as

---

[14] Johann Wolfgang Von Goethe, <u>Wilhelm Meister's Apprenticeship</u>, Book 5, Chapter 1, 1786-1830.

you will note in later Chapters, for the purpose of reflecting on the significance of the matter being discerned, for stepping back, as it were, and contemplating the mystery beginning to unfold. Poetry may trigger the group to move toward other options because imaginations are sparked by new insights. Or, a particular poem may "bless" the group at a specific juncture in its dialogue or in its culminating decision. "The world is charged with the grandeur of God ... There lives the dearest freshness deep down things...[15] Poetry can help us hear, then speak, to the depth of an issue--the "deep down things"--in spiritual discernment. The Jesuit poet, Gerard Manley Hopkins, names all of creation as sacramental, as charged with loving reminders of the nearness of God. So, the inclusion of poetry in a discernment process can help discerners discover and uncover ideas, can help them continue in the process with newfound energy.

In 1975, the Catholic Bishops of Appalachia wrote a pastoral message on powerlessness in response to the cries of the Appalachian people. *This Land is Home to Me* reads like an epic poem. It mirrors the history and art of the people of Appalachia with the history of God's salvific action in the world. It reminds its readers to look at the faith-life of artists, but also at the artistic life of the faithful. It suggests that each parish develop a "center of popular culture" no matter what their economic situation. This was certainly quite a challenge! In their closing words, the Bishops wrote:

"In taking up [the weak things of this world],
hopefully the Church
might once again
be known as
- a center of the Spirit,
- a place where poetry dares to speak,
- where the song reigns unchallenged,
- where art flourishes,
- where nature is welcome,
- where little people [children] and little needs come first,
- where justice speaks loudly,

---

[15] Helen Gardner, ed. "God's Grandeur", <u>Oxford Book of English Mystical Verse</u>. London: Oxford University Press, p 786.

21

*- where in a wilderness of idolatrous destruction the great
voice of God still cries
out for life."[16]*

Our churches, regardless of denomination, can be known as "a center of the Spirit." This will happen if leadership is provided to engage people in their history (stories), if leadership provides and encourages opportunities for artistic expressions to be gradually uncovered. Poetry used in spiritual discernment can certainly be that of published authors, or be composed by the persons engaged in spiritual discernment.

Haiku, an unrhymed Japanese lyric poem having a fixed three-line form containing five, seven and five syllables respectively, a form that requires no meter or rhyming, can be rather easily written by persons of all ages. Discernmentarians can extend an invitation to write Haiku to participants in a discernment process. Words or phrases are all that is needed. Invite inner feelings to come forth. There are no wrong words. Let this creative time be followed this by a time of silence spent outdoors, or anywhere of the persons' choosing.

When persons share their Haiku poems, respectful silence is an appropriate response. So are words of praise or an announced sung refrain such as "Spirit of the Living God, fall afresh on me..."[17] from the hymn, "Spirit of the Living God." So is transferring the poem onto paper in the form of Oriental calligraphy, i.e. Shodo (Japanese Brush Calligraphy).

Not every person will find that writing a poem, especially one to be shared, is easy. Sometimes the focus for a poem that comes to mind is deeply rooted in a personal fear, or is buried in one's grief or pain. Writing a poem does, however, have the potential for achieving a catharsis, or personal transformation. God is to be found in that process. Note how that happened in the following poem by Emily Brown:

"The flame is no longer held within the chamber

---

[16] Catholic Bishops of Appalachia. This Land is Home to Me. Webster Springs, WV: Catholic Committee of Appalachia, 1990.

[17] Daniel Iverson, Spirit of the Living God, The Presbyterian Hymnal, (Louisville, KY: Westminster/John Knox Press, 1990). No.322.

it burns everywhere
We are on fire
Children everywhere
Seeking water that will heal
The holy water
That is clear
Water unpolluted
But everywhere there is dirt and dust
That has settled into and poisoned the streams
Deep, deep down in the earth
There is pure water
The way is down
The old sources have become clogged
New wells are sought
And sounding bar, divining rods, of every kind
Are held over the sands of our time
In efforts to discern the new watering places
That might be there
Deep down
For us

I have met her
That one
Who holds a true divining rod
That one who is seeking pure water."[18]

The relationship that we come to understand between our faith and our creativity, is linked to our desire to explore and understand mystery -- the unknown -- and to achieve personal transformation, as well as interconnectedness. Our task as poets and writers, as followers of our inner and deeper voices, is to push the boundaries of known language to its limits. It is to use what we know to describe that which has no obvious shape or form. This profound task is, I believe, meant to provide us with just a glimpse into the mystery of God.

This Native American poem is found in *Earth Prayers from around the World:*

---

[18] Emily Brown, "The Burning Bush," Well of Living Waters, Rhoda Head, ed et al. Los Angeles, CA: C. G. Jung Institute of Los Angeles, 1977.

"Now Talking God
Beauty is before me
And beauty is behind me.
Above and below me
hovers the beautiful.
I am surrounded by it.
I am immersed in it.
In my youth I am aware of it.
And in my old age I shall walk quietly
The beautiful trail." [19]

Dare I say that how we live will determine the type of poetry we create? I believe that poets (each of us are poets in some manner) whose hearts are concerned about being faithful in seeking God's yearning in our lives, will create art in ways that are insightful and inspiring. The circumstances of our personal lives may at various times be dark or dismal, yet if God's yearning is our focus, our writings will express a balance of darkness and light.

As a discernmentarian, I have prepared small scrolls containing a short Scripture passage or lines of a poem. I then invited each person to randomly choose one from a basket. After taking some personal quiet time to ponder the meaning of the particular passage for one's own life and/or for the life of the group, I invited any sharing participants wished to offer the group. (There are no wrong comments.) -- A follow-up exercise might be to ask participants to reflect on the complete passage of Scripture, or the complete poem, before the next gathering, and come prepared to offer more extensive reflections to the group.

Jesus' words, passed down to us in written traditions, were often phrased in a poetic way. Note 2 Corinthians 17:18: "My grace is enough for you; for power is at full strength in weakness." Or, John 15:1-10: "Whoever remains in me...bears fruit in plenty...cut off from

---

[19] Elizabeth Roberts and Elias Amidon, eds. Earth Prayers from around the World: 365 Prayers, Poems and Invocations for Honoring the Earth. San Francisco, CA: Harper Collins, 1991. p 32.

me you can do nothing." Or, Luke 8:4-15: Jesus cried "Anyone who has ears for listening should listen...people with a noble and generous heart who have heard the word and take it to themselves yield a harvest." What particular Scripture passages will speak to the experience of your particular group? Be alert to the poetic and scriptural offerings of the participants in spiritual discernment.

In Mary Benet McKinney's book, *Sharing Wisdom, A Process For Group Decision Making,* she includes a wonderful poem by Chuck Lathrop, a contemporary American poet currently living in Ireland. The poem is entitled *In Search of a Round Table.* I have used this poem in a number of settings, including a process of spiritual discernment. It speaks to the shared wisdom model of church, a model in which everyone is included and respected for the wisdom they bring to the table. Lest this description sounds too idealistic, the poem addresses all the re-sizing, changing and arranging that needs to happen until the table becomes like a round table for worship.

Two additional poetry resources for a discernmentarian are: *Mantras from a Poet: Jessica Powers,* by Robert F. Morneau, highlighting fifteen of Jessica Powers' poems with illustrations, short musical mantras and commentaries that share insights into the poetry's rich symbols, and *Clay Vessels and Other Poems* by John McNamee, which captures in poetry the irony, tragedy and beauty that is hidden even among the shambles of desolate urban neighborhoods. In this book, artist Robert McGovern's woodcuts reflect the awe and ordeal that McNamee's poetry reveals.

ICONS

Although icons are mostly associated with Russian painting, the very first icons were actually made in Greece between the First and Third Centuries AD. The word icon is Greek too, meaning likeness or image. Icons from the Sixth Century onward were extremely important in Orthodox worship and teaching. In the Eighth Century their usage came into question. Iconoclasts opposed their use, reasoning that they perverted the worship of God. They demanded their removal and didn't hesitate to use force and destruction in the process. Leo III issued a proclamation in the year 730 forbidding the use of icons in public worship, so their continued use depended upon the whim of the current Emperor. In 843, on the first Sunday of Lent, icons were restored to their original place in Eastern worship.

To the modern eye, a Byzantine image usually suggests a stiff, stylized figure. But in their own time, icons were true portraits -- faces, bodies and costumes authenticated through visions and dreams. They were inspired. They portrayed movement and emotion.

During the Byzantine era, the Russians created a very ornate icon style that serves as a model for contemporary icon-making. Painted and engraved, then adorned with enamel, filigree and jewels, some modern icons recreate traditional Russian styles and symbols, thereby attempting to share the mystery of medieval spirituality. Today, regardless of one's personal religious beliefs, or lack of familiarity with icons, they can be instrumental in leading us into the mystery of the Divine.

The late Henri Nouwen, in his book entitled *Behold The Beauty Of The Lord: Praying With Icons*, wrote of his growing attraction to icons. He chose to focus on this particular art form "because they are created for the sole purpose of offering access, through the gate of the visible, to the mystery of the invisible. Icons are painted to lead us into the inner room of prayer and bring us close to the heart of God."[20] For his book, Nouwen chose these particular icons: *the Holy Trinity, the Virgin of Vladimir, the Savior of Zvenigorod,* and the *Descent of the Holy Spirit*. Each one of these icons expresses a particular aspect of the mystery of our salvation.

There is no doubt that Renaissance, as well as contemporary artists, know how to invite the gazer *into* the picture. Icons are meant for contemplating, as their mystery is not revealed just upon first glance. Each time one engages with an icon, there is an invitation to enter a new space that is created *between* the icon and the person gazing at it. When a sequence of time is spent with the same icon, God is continually revealed in a myriad of ways. The time this takes, which could be hours, days, months or years, serves to create and deepen a space within oneself that is known as prayer. The icon calls one to reflect upon what it means to be holy, and how one should live out the image of God that is revealed in the icon.

The use of icons need never be limited to personal prayer,

---

[20] Henri Nouwen. Behold The Beauty Of The Lord: Praying With Icons. Notre Dame, IN: Ave Maria Press, 1987, p 14.

though this is their most common usage. A discernmentarian can introduce an icon into group spiritual discernment rather effectively. Since the discernmentarian is also a gazer who waits and listens for the Spirit's guidance, you invite the group into silent reflection before a particular icon. The icon should be placed so that everyone in the group can see it completely, and so there are no surrounding distractions. Call the group into quiet with some background centering music that causes everyone to set aside distractions and focus on the simple, calming melody. Follow this centering time with a reverent sharing of insights into that which has been gazed upon: "What did you notice about this icon?" The discerners may be hesitant at first, but all their comments should be considered helpful to the group. They are sure to see different things.

It may help the group to become more familiar with the icon to return to another time of silence following the comments made above. Then ask the same question: "What did you notice?" followed by your own questions leading further into Biblical or theological reflection, e.g., "I noticed...", "I wonder..." Attempt to key your questions to the matter for discernment so that personal and communal ramifications of the issue will reach a deeper level of contemplation during the continuing Movements of spiritual discernment.

This art form may take some getting used to if persons in spiritual discernment are totally unfamiliar with icons, but the icons otherness usually engages imaginations, invites dialogue, and leads the group into deeper insights. Icons are "written", as Eastern Christian iconographers say, to help us go deeper.

Novalis, a Canadian publishing house (P.O. Box 216, Rousss Point, NY, 12979-9931; 1-800-387-7164) prints inexpensive, yet beautiful, icon calendars each year. The 1997 calendar, *Contemplating the Mystery,* is rich in Rublev's Fourteenth and Fifteenth Century icon masterpieces. (The calendar section is perforated for easy removal.) Discernmentarians might begin their own modest collection of icons for use in spiritual discernment in this inexpensive way.

Jim Forest's *Praying With Icons* is a primer on the background of icons and their position in the Oxthodox tradition. He defines icons as aids to, even servants of, those who pray. Short chapters cover the making of icons, rules and prayers for iconographers, and the significance of color and symbols that icons have in common.

The major portion of Forest's book deals with specific icons, detailing the theology behind the representations. Each of the icons are treated as old friends, as confidantes on the journey, as companions in the art of contemplative prayer. The commentaries are obviously the fruit of reflection over years of praying with his eyes. We can do the same, individually, or as a group in spiritual discernment.

Twenty-eight contemporary icons of Mary, the mother of God, are found in *Mary, Mother of My Lord*, by Christine Granger, a Canadian artist whose work is found in many public and private collections, including the Canadian Museum of Civilization. Her full color icons are accompanied by both traditional and contemporary prayers and hymns. This book is also a Novalis publication.

What would, in any case, be a very valuable book of biographies of saintly persons becomes a spiritual classic with the addition of Robert Lentz's icons. *A Passion for Life: Fragments of the Face of God*, by Joan Chittister, is an Orbis Books publication, 1996. Chittister's expansive collection of meditations on the lives of persons who have been faithful to God ranges from Eve, *The Image of God*, to the University Martyrs, *Icons of the Patience of God*, and from Julian of Norwich, *Icon of the Motherhood of God*, to Martin Luther King, Jr., *The Icon of Light in Darkness*. Robert Lentz, a native of Colorado and the grandson of Russian immigrants, has spent considerable time in a Greek monastery as an apprentice to a master iconographer. His icons are of holy men and women without regard to their religious affiliation, thus enabling persons of varied cultures to share in the rich tradition of the Byzantine East. Lentz also continues to respond to persons wishing to commission an original icon. I have no doubt that this book by Lentz and Chittister can aid discerners in sorting out the ambiguities and paradoxes that surface during the process of spiritual discernment, especially if the framed issue is obviously related to the spirituality of any of the Twentieth Century personages included in this text.

Sometimes because of our physical or mental limitations, we can be numb or absent-minded, unprepared to be present to the mystery of an icon unfolding before us. When this happens we are probably not vulnerable enough, not capable of looking beyond appearances, or moving from our visible reality to the invisible reality. This is part of being human. But, when we are ready, we can be taken by surprise! As was Moses, who was roaming the countryside with his flocks when suddenly a bush appeared on the horizon, a bush on fire, yet not consumed. Moses' attentiveness to what he saw changed him. He was

still the same ordinary sheepherder, but his life took on new meaning.
There is a Thirteenth Century icon in the Monastery of St.
Catherine in Egypt that depicts Moses before the burning bush. Helen
Dudar writes the following about this particular icon, a photograph of
which is included in the same article: "Amid the borrowed treasures to
be seen right now at the Metropolitan Museum of Art in New York is a
painted image of a blond lad. He has a stylized face you will never
encounter in your neighborhood McDonald's and a long body that seems
boneless and weightless. Towering over a rocky, surreal landscape, he is
leaning into feathery flames that could be mistaken for a burst of red
ferns, and removing his sandals on God's command to set his feet
unshod on holy ground. Behind him is sky, not blue sky of course, but a
lush reach of burnished gold. We stand in the presence of Moses before
the Burning Bush, a *literal* presence meant to remind the believer of the
power and truth of the Bible. That familiar icon exudes a familiar
intensity, a fervor that may also strike us on first encountering unfamiliar
or alien examples of unconquerable faith--a commanding African tribal
carving of a figure of worship, perhaps, or an Edward Hicks offering of
tranquil beats in one of is beguiling celebrations of the "Peaceable
Kingdom." They all insist on the possibility of life without doubt."[21]
    It is this is kind of in depth meaning we search for when we
prayerfully gaze deeper into an icon.

PAINTINGS

    Art, incorporated into spiritual discernment, should nourish,
challenge and call forth our best efforts toward the transformed
consciousness we seek. As long as the nobility of the artist or the history
of a painting doesn't get in the way of reflection, paintings, great
masterpieces or otherwise, can be used for silent reflection followed by
sharing of insights during spiritual discernment. Paintings can be
religious or secular. The objective in using any type of visual art is to
probe for God's presence and message within it. They should not
detract in any way from God's presence or message.

---

[21] Helen Dudar, "The faith of the Byzantine world is alive at the Met",
Smithsonian Magazine, April, 1997, p 101.

Should you choose to use a painting which has trees or a forest in it, such as Claude Monet's *Giverny* (1925/1926), a litmus test for appropriateness could be what Jessica Powers says well in her poem "The Mercy of God": *"I walked out of myself and went into the woods of God's mercy, and here I abide."*[22] Does the painting lead you into God's presence? Helen Dudar writes "...every work of art, even an abstract painting, has a subject beyond the painter's enslavement to an inner vision. Monet needed vistas in which the sun burned the earth, flicked across the sea, yellowed the sky, bronzed the leaves. ...Joachim Pissarro calls Monet "a pictorial digger."[23] Our charge is to be pictorial diggers, actively involved in gazing for the deeper meanings.

The use of any of Degas' paintings of one or more ballet dancers, or Monet's "Blue Waterlilies", "The Artist's Garden At Giverny", or "Three Figures Under Lilacs", can disclose patterns, isolate elements, and help individuals focus on the matter for discernment. A Picasso composition with craggy geometric shapes can help identify a tension between the known and the new in spiritual discernment.

"Red Kapok Blossoms", by Chao Shao-An, done in ink and colors on paper in 1970, shows a strong tree trunk with an opening on one side that could have been the result of age or inclement weather. It has delicate red and yellow flowers softly cascading from top branches and a single bid hovering in flight by the tree. All aspects of this artwork are ripe for reflection during discernment, e.g., "Like the trunk, what is our strength, and what is our weakness?"

Contemplating one of Georges Seurat's paintings using the technique of pointillism, the application of paint in small dot and brush strokes, can lead one to see the picture as a whole, from a distance -- the very process we embark on when we begin spiritual discernment. We move from single points of energy, or light, into the whole picture.

I was very excited to come across the article "Creating a Watercolor Journal Using Meditation" by Linda S. Price in the May, 1997 American Artist magazine. The author wrote about Maureen Carey, who works with inner-city homeless people in Brooklyn, New York, and Carey's experience of painting with watercolors during times

---

[22] Regina Siegfried, Robert Morneau, eds. Selected Poetry of Jessica Powers. Kansas City, MO: Sheed & Ward, 1989, p 133.

[23] Helen Dudar, "When light meets water, Monet on the Mediterranean", Smithsonian Magazine, July, 1997, p 83.

of personal meditation. Carey believes that for her there is a link between meditation and creativity: "It presents me with the time to simply be and to process my life. It makes me aware I'm not the center of the universe. It enables me to know myself more deeply and opens me up to how God is present in my life and work. Getting lost in meditation is very much like losing yourself during the painting process. I'm a very logical person, the kind who likes to make outlines, and meditation releases me to a more intuitive, free-flowing place."[24]

One of Carey's works, "Alive in Mystery", struck me in particular because of its mystical quality. It's almost like she was painting outside of her own pre-established lines. Unlike other Carey paintings displayed in the article, this painting could be, for me, much more than at first glance. What appears to be a bright sun does not have the traditional circle shape, for example. It isn't as well defined a landscape as another illustrated favorite of mine, "Peaceful Listening", a 1995 9x6 ink and watercolor.

If painting is a natural or a to-be-tried creative medium for persons in spiritual discernment, what could be better than keeping an artistic journal during the process of discernment? This journal will be as unique as each individual artist. It can be shared according to the artists' wishes, and worked on during the gatherings as well as between times.

Carey has created a workshop on the connections between spirituality, meditation and art. As one component of the workshop, she has the entire group take turns creating a painting, each artist passing on the brush to another at the sound of a bell. Carey's goal is that each person leaves the workshop with "an understanding that art is a process, not a product."[25]

If a discernmentarian were to propose such a creation, what might be some possible outcomes from this activity? I predict these as potential, though not all encompassing, outcomes: 1) the artwork, like the process of spiritual discernment, will begin to take on a life of its own as soon as the group takes on a kindred spirit; 2) creating the art will happen at directed, as well as spontaneous times; 3) the artists will add onto, as well as refine, each other's efforts in the process; and 4) the art

---

[24] Linda S. Price, "Creating a Watercolor Journal Using Meditation", American Artist, May, 1997, BPI Communications, p. 55,57.
[25] Ibid, p. 81.

will reflect the joys and tensions within the discernment group, perhaps very well outsizing the initial dimensions of the canvas.

Spiritual discernment is like that, too. It may cause participants to paint both inside and outside their own preset "lines." A process of spiritual discernment will intentionally lead discerners into intuitive, free-flowing space. This free-flowing, creative space will be highlighted most notably during the Movements of Listening, Exploring and Improving in following Chapters.

The Viennese artist Gustav Klimt (1862-1918) executed "Death and Life", oil on canvas, in 1908 and 1911. It is in the collection of Marietta Preleuthner in Saltzburg. "The painting is quite typically Symbolist in both content and form. Bright colors, mosaic-like or enamel-like, stud the surfaces that enwrap the voluptuously somnolent figures in the *Life* group, in which intertwined images of infancy, youth, maturity, and old age celebrate life as bound up with love. ... The tableau of defenseless sleep is set off against the specter of *Death*, the nocturnal assassin, who advances threateningly upon it. The shroud of the fleshless *Death* is appropriately dark as night, only dimly decked with funeral black crosses and chiromatic symbols. While *Life*, sated with love, sleeps, its enemy, *Death*, wakes."[26]

What would happen if a discernmentarian displayed this painting at the group's first gathering time, using it for theological reflection throughout the process of discernment? I can imagine vivid and profound sharing on the meaning of moving from infancy to maturity in decision making, on death-dealing and life-giving rituals participants have experienced, on hopes and dreams about fulfilling the mission of the group, etc. An experience of this kind could cause the group to grow in spiritual friendship not only with the painting, but as a group.

I have had a favorite painting since the days of my childhood. It is Georges Seurat's (1859-1891) "La Grande Jatte", housed in the Art Institute of Chicago as part of the Helen Birch Bartlett Memorial Collection. It is said that the free and fluent play of color in this work was disciplined into a calculated arrangement by prior rules of design accepted and imposed by the artist. The pattern in "La Grande Jatte" is based on vertical figures and trees, the horizontals of shadows and the distant embankment, and the diagonals in the shadows and shoreline,

---

[26]Richard G. Tansey, Fred S. Kleiner. Gardner's Art Through the Ages. Fort Worth, TX: Harcourt Brace College Publishers, 1996, p. 1036.

each of which contributes to the wonderful effect of this painting.

Seurat carved out a deep rectangular space in this picture. It is as if one is looking a mile down the river from where one is standing. The picture is filled with sunshine and everything is coherent in precise organization: women with parasols, men in top hats, children in their Sunday best, dogs looking for picnic morsels, sailboat and rowing teams.

As a child, I remember making up stories about the life circumstances of many of the characters in this painting. As an adult, I've forgone that activity for the simple pleasure of amazement over the paintings' construction. The depth of the scene, the shadows and the many small details contributing to the whole, still catch me by surprise.

Paintings can help us uncover what we care for deeply, what charms us unduly, and what we may need to eliminate from our lives. They can put us in touch with our cultures and customs, our values, our fears and rigidities. They can point us toward a place where God's Spirit is at work. Little did I think this was happening to me as I've reflected on Seurat's composition over the years. But now I can see that my musings have done just that!

During the Movements of spiritual discernment, there is ample time and use for growing in amazement with the composition of a painting. A process of discernment is one of moving from small pieces of information, their details and the shadows that exist, into the whole picture. So, discernment is basically a process parallel to the completion of a painting: a focus is discerned (framed), parameters are determined, unnecessary and extraneous materials are set aside and the focus is deepened, explored and improved upon until the work is completed.

It might be very helpful for the group to agree upon one painting (or icon) to "sit with" throughout a discernment process. See how the artwork grows on the group, becomes richer and more significant to them. -- You will find more ideas on following pages. Just know that you can't do everything during one process of spiritual discernment!

A particular season of the church year might warrant a choice such as Piero della Francesca's Fifteenth Century painting of the "Resurrection" as an artistic focus a discernment process. While housed in the Pinacoteca Comunale in Sansepolcro, Italy, it is available in smaller prints. The painting shows four tired guards, in varied poses, on the side of Jesus' tomb. Jesus stands wide-eyed on the other side, with one foot in the sarcophagus (stone coffin) and the other resting on top of its open edge. He holds a staff, the sign of a triumphal victory over

33

death. The artwork is keyed to Matthew 28: 4-6, in which the angel tells the women not to be afraid, for Jesus has been raised from the dead.

The longer I gaze at this print the more I see. The landscape to the left contains trees devoid of foliage, but the landscape on the right is verdant with life. The four sleeping guards, unaware of what has happened, take on unique personalities. And, Jesus himself offers food for thought. His posture, his expression, and his placement within the painting all lead me into reflection -- and if I stay with the painting long enough, into prayer. Some questions for reflection geared to this particular painting are: "What opportunities currently in your path are distractions from seeing the situation as it truly is?" "How might you trouble yourself to get up and moving on Jesus' behalf?" "What would be the deeper change in your/our lives?" Answers to such questions may lead to a firmer grappling with the matter for discernment, and could contribute to a positive change of heart about the matter.

The Cleveland Museum of Art has one of the longest surviving landscapes, a hanging scroll, ink on paper, by Tung Ch'i-Ch'ang (1555-1636) called "The Ch'ing Mountain, 1617." The foreground and far distance are fairly logical and understandable. The middle section is irrational and perplexing. Tung, like Twentieth Century cubist painters, seems to depict simultaneously both the interior and exterior of the geological formations, creating multiple views of a simple mountain.

While gazing at this magnificent scroll, I became transported into the heights and depths of the mountain, into the acres of immense vegetation, and onto barren rocks. I could drink from a stream, observe imaginary critters, feel a tiredness in my bones from bodily exertion and glory in the view of distant mountains. Some questions could be asked of discerners pondering this scroll: "Where are you on your journey in spiritual discernment?" "Where are we?" "What stands as obstacles on our journey?" "Who is on the road with us?"

At the time Tung painted this hanging scroll, his own world was in a state of disorder. One year earlier, his estate had been burned by angry rioters. During the following years, Tung lived on a boat with friends, finding solace in their companionship. He ended his painting with this inscription: "In the splendor of autumn, where is the most worthy spot to spend the day? Amid the rustling sounds of mountain streams, with a volume in hand, meditating on the Tao."[27]

You might ask: "Where is your 'most worthy spot' during spiritual discernment?" "What is becoming sacred space for you between the gathering times, a space for your ongoing personal prayer and reflection?" "What icon, painting, sculpture do you resonate with and where are you in the picture?" "What volume do you have in hand?"

Landscape art by any medium, watercolor, ink on paper or silk, oil painting, etc., may provide thought-provoking questions during spiritual discernment. Note the picture's space, structure and sense of balance. Note how each element relates to the others. "Is there energy or vitality?" "What is dominant?" "Where is the composition closed or open?" Ruminate over your response to these questions individually and as a group.

During spiritual discernment, discerners need a rhythm of silence. Some paintings employ a sense of beauty where empty space seems, at first glance, to dominate over substance. When discovered, this is to be treasured. Likewise, we can learn to appreciate where abrupt stylistic shifts occur within a single form, where there is seeming illogic, incoherence and instability at every turn. Both assist the process.

To be discovered in the process of reflecting on a work of art is how the piece is unified overall. "What is the deeper beauty, and what is its unity?" "Where and how do you spiritually resonate with this particular artwork?" Let the art become your text, become a visionary poem. Let it lead you into spiritual insight.

Handpainted Chinese handscrolls such as "Clearing after Snow on Mountain Passes" by Tung Ch'i-Ch'ang, ordinarily on display at the Beijing Palace Museum, was a delightful part of *The Century of Tung Ch'i-Ch'ang*, a touring exhibition of treasures from China in 1992. This handscroll depicts a configuration of wide-stretching cloud-filled mountains and is simply breathtaking. Horizontal handscrolls such as this are viewed from right to left. Viewers need look at only a cubic foot or so at a time because the compositions are carefully constructed to be viewed this way. Chinese handscrolls introduce an element that rarely exists in Western paintings -- that of progression through time. A process of spiritual discernment is likewise, a progression through time.

Certain seasons of the church year also lend themselves to the

---

[27] Smithsonian Institution, *The Ch'ing-pien Mountain*, 1617, Hanging Scroll, ink on paper, The Cleveland Museum of Art.

use of sacred art. Think of the Christmas season, and some of the beautiful nativity masterpieces. There is a medieval nativity painting on oakwood by Melchior Broederlam (d. 1409). There is a Seventeenth Century painting by G. B. Castiglione which hangs in the Louvre in Paris. Perhaps you have a Christmas card, or a print, of one of these, or yet another, masterpiece? I invite you to use it for personal meditation, then offer it to the group in discernment for contemplation and reflection.

During the season of Lent, discerners might choose to reflect on one of countless paintings of the Last Supper depicting Jesus seated at table with the twelve apostles, or washing their feet. Then too, there is an abundance of medieval and contemporary art surrounding the Easter season. In "Appearing to the Apostles after the Resurrection", painted just before the Nineteenth Century by William Blake and on display at the Yale Center for British Art, the light surrounding Jesus clearly looks supernatural. Yet the wounds on his hands and on his side show that he is the historical Jesus whom the disciples knew. A discernmentarian might ask: "What feelings stir inside you while reflecting on this painting?" "What do you/we need to do to contribute to a better way of life for others?" "Are you/we willing to do this even if it means we might not be understood?"

Tapping into centuries of religious art and into the church year, discernmentarians can facilitate new discoveries about the life and teachings of Jesus, and delve deeper into their own hearts as they search for God's yearning for them.

PHOTOGRAPHY

New York Times photographer Chester Higgins, Jr., has, for the past thirty years, traveled around the world documenting the traditions, spirituality and dignity of people of African heritage. Some two hundred seventy of his photographs were displayed in the South Gallery of the Arts and Industries Building of the Smithsonian early in 1997. "It's the people's characters themselves speaking through the film, through the lens that tells the story,"[28] says Higgins.

---

[28] Diane M. Bolz, "Picturing the face of the African diaspora," Smithsonian Magazine, February, 1997, p 26.

One of his photographs, displayed in the February, 1997 issue of Smithsonian Magazine, shows a striking facial portrait of a Muslim woman in Brooklyn, New York. Her head, face and neck are all draped in white. Only her eyes and the top of her nose are undraped. I tend to view this photograph as an icon because her eyes are so expressive and seem to literally, look me in the eyes.

Another black and white photograph in the same magazine entitled "Migratory Cotton Picker, Eloy, Arizona", by Dorothea Lange, taken in 1940, shows a man's face covered from the nose down by a left hand with the palm forward. That hand has obviously born the heat of the day and is scarred from hours of hard labor. A discernmentarian might follow the display of this photo with a question such as: "What does this photograph tell us about the labor of spiritual discernment?"

A good source book among many standard photography reference books, is *A World History of Photography*, first published in 1984 by art historian Naomi Rosenblum. It is filled with photographs of people and places from many cultures. You might choose a particular photograph to use in spiritual discernment as you would a painting, icon, etc., or the book may spark in you the idea to find a poignant photo or slide you have in a treasured collection. Just remember that the chosen work needs universal appeal. It needs to speak beyond your personal interpretation or memories. It needs to be able to prompt reflection on the matter for discernment, so it needs to resonate with the group. Likewise, members of the group may contribute photos that will assist the group in discerning its values and its unfinished story.

I've had the experience of being part of gathering to which each participant brought a photograph of his/her individual sacred space, a place that resonated within as a "spiritual home". (Of course we were informed to do this in plenty of time.) Some persons brought pictures of favorite places at the seashore, others of chapel spaces, others of family cabins in the woods or in the mountains. After each photograph and its story was shared and reverenced, we displayed the photographs as in a mandala, defined as a wheel of life, a diagram of the cosmos, or the cycle of being and becoming. Our group displayed the photographs in one large circle on a cloth banner. (The same could be done on paper or any other material.) Our large group gave this title to our mandala: "Sacred Spaces: Something New Is Unfolding." Think about the possibility of creating a discernment group mandala as you read further about the specific Movements in the process of spiritual discernment.

There is a Sierra Club book entitled *Women in the Material World* by photojournalist, Peter Menzal, and former TV news producer, Faith D'Aluisio. The book contains over three hundred color photographs. Six of these photos are shown in the article "Disarmingly Natural" in the March, 1997 (Vol. 71, No. 3) issue of *Popular Photography*. The magazine article first caught my attention because of its title, then because of the five delightful photographs included in the short article. I was struck by making this mental connection with the process of spiritual discernment: God's Spirit leads in ways that are "disarmingly natural." Discerners are led by the Spirit of God through the process to a decision that is God's natural yearning, and sometimes we are taken by surprise. In a process of spiritual discernment we disarm ourselves by letting go of our own wills and seeking God's yearning -- nothing more -- but this journey is not so much our work, as the gift of God's Spirit at work.

The use of cinema is another possibility for a process of spiritual discernment. A video may be too lengthy to watch as a group. If that is the case, discerners could view the selection on their own. Yet, the value of engaging in a video together might well prompt consideration of a longer timeframe within which to meet.

The movie *Babette's Feast*, written and directed by Gabriel Axel, and distributed in the United States by Orion Pictures Corporation, is a story of building community with a most unlikely group. The film explores the complex relationship between human physical and spiritual needs. Babette, a French expatriot, lives an austere lifestyle in Denmark and works for room and board in the household of two sisters. The sisters are spiritual leaders of a small religious sect established by their father. Upon learning that she had won the lottery, Babette asks permission of the sisters to cook a real French dinner. With their approval, Babette imports everything necessary for the feast, from food to table settings. As the story progresses, viewers watch a scrumptious meal being prepared and the films' characters develop. While most of the characters speak very little, an invited guest talks eloquently about the spiritual nature of the meal and the care with which it has been prepared and served. It is this character who is able to reflect deeply upon the presence of God as the greatest gift in the midst of human community. His words have communion overtones. This man speaks, in ordinary conversational style, of shedding past disagreements and exploring options for realizing the group's potential.

If your discernment group is grappling with what "community" means, or how important its formation is in their discernment process, this film will make some powerful points and cause much food-for-thought and dialogue. This movie has shown in fine arts theaters throughout the States, and the video is available from Franciscan Communications in Los Angeles, California. Its use would be appropriate during any of the Movements of spiritual discernment discussed in future Chapters. As discernmentarian, you may wish to view this video in preparation for your ministry.

Another film, produced in 1991 and released on video in 1992 by Keynote Video, is Julie Dash's *Daughters of the Dust*. It is the story, significantly portrayed in black and white, of an African American family journeying north at the turn of the Twentieth Century. The hardships they experienced and yet their deep care for one another speak well to the struggles we all experience in discerning right choices.

Another videotape suitable for viewing as a group is entitled *Mother Earth*, by Terre Nash. Eleven minutes long, it is available from the National Film Board of Canada. It is a poetic film about the recurring patterns of life, death, and rebirth in nature as well as culture. During times of disagreement, or as one or more discerners struggle with letting go of their preconceived notions about the outcome of the discernment process, it can be helpful to get in touch with the larger picture of nature and its struggles with the life cycle. This usually helps put things in better perspective. Sometimes taking a long walk will do the same, but if circumstances don't permit that, try this video or one like it.

The autumn, 1996 issue of Initiatives in Religion, contained an article entitled "The Arts in Theological Education." Various books and videotapes were reviewed, but I quickly noticed that the video *Looking For God*, has potential use in a process of spiritual discernment. This is how the video is described: "It contains four segments that challenge viewers to consider a variety of historical and traditional images as nourishment for faith. With images from the ancient world of painting and sculpture along with contemporary visuals from advertising, the video promotes development of insights and critical skills to enhance faith development. The video is divided into four segments. *Looking for God in the Human Face* suggests that images can lead us to an authentic view of ourselves and God; *Looking for God in the Human Form* takes Christ's incarnation as the catalyst for examining how the human body is presented in advertising; *Looking for God in Nature* prompts the viewer to reflect on nature's terrors as well as its peacefulness in order to understand God as Creator; *Looking for God in Mystery* challenges viewers to understand that all representation of God in inadequate to the task and shows how artists attempt to take us beyond our own strivings."[29] When we move into consideration of the specific Movements in spiritual discernment, it will become apparent how reflection on the human face, the human form, nature and mystery can be artfully integrated into a process.

A good Hispanic resource for a discernmentarian is *The Word Becomes Flesh - Danzando Con Crecion*, featuring Martha Ann Kirk, with music by Rufino Zaragosa. This video explores the pastoral values of using the arts, particularly drama and dance, in prayer. Produced by Incarnate Word College, it is available from Sheed & Ward Publishing Company and is fifty-six minutes in length.

Margaret Wheatley's video about her book *Leadership and the New Science*, has stunning visuals. Wheatley applies the science of chaos, the "footprints of chaos", as well as quantum mechanics and field theory of modern physics to the dynamics of organizations. Her premise is that if we learn how nature operates, we can better embrace nature. Wheatley says that fractals appear everywhere in nature. They are the repeating patterns of organization that gives shape to clouds, snowflakes, flowers and vegetables. A fractal repeats a similar pattern of design at ever smaller levels of scale.

To illustrate this, look at a head of broccoli. The dominant shape of the head is repeated in the makeup of the elements that join each other to form a single floret. Scientists believe this happens because even though there is freedom of development at any given moment in response to a variety of factors, the final shape is determined by pre-existing parameters.

Think about what you know of spiritual discernment in light of Wheatley's premise: 1) chaos is a route to order and allows us to reach a higher level of creativity; 2) information informs and forms us; it is the primary organizing force, or information made visible; 3) relationships are at the heart of reality; they energize us and connect us; and 4) a vision surrounds us like the invisible fields operating in our universe; we can and do influence and energize each other.

---

[29] Lilly Endowment, Inc., "The Arts in Theological Education", Initiatives in Religion, Autumn, 1996, pp 7-8.

In spiritual discernment, the final shape is determined by pre-existing parameters: grounded in a Guiding Principle and with freedom to develop the best option possible, the process moves forward under the guidance of God's Spirit. Would you like further discussion of this premise and its' implications for spiritual discernment? Subsequent Chapters will deal with chaos, creativity, information, relationships and vision.

MOSAICS

Mosaics created throughout the centuries are available for a process of spiritual discernment. Copies of many mosaic originals are available in poster-size reprints, in photographs in a myriad of art history books, and they are even available in bookstores and museums as postcards or bookmarks.

Mosaic is an art form consisting of colored pieces of glass (called *tesserae* in Latin) pressed into soft plaster to form pictures. Such art was widely used for decoration in the Byzantine Church in Italy during the so-called Italo-Byzantine period. The construction of monumental churches with mosaics of Christ began in Rome, Jerusalem, Constantinople and Milan with the reign of Constantine in the Fourth Century. By the Sixth Century, the same was true of Ravenna. This art depicted dogma and conciliar pronouncements. Examples of these include the fifth-century mosaic of Christ enthroned and flanked by the apostles in Santa Pudenziana and the fifth-century Marian mosaic at St. Mary Major following the Council of Ephesus of 431 that affirmed Mary as *Theotokos*, Mother of God. Such images, rooted in an imperial culture, exist to the present day. This points to an important facet of religious art: its materials and media, its use of symbols and conceptual metaphors convey the particularities of Christian peoples in individual cultures, historical periods, and regions even as the art strives to embody the more universal truths of redemption in Christ for all humanity.

The technique for cloisonne enameling was brought to China by missionaries from central Asia sometime in the mid-Fourteenth Century. Smithsonian catalogues are one source for purchasing exquisite examples of cloisonne art. One piece I especially admire is called the "Majestic Cloisonne Phoenix", intricately plumed and beautifully rendered in brilliant, hand-applied enamels. The phoenix is perched atop a carved rosewood-finished base from which blooms a cloisonne blossom. There is much "movement" in this particular art piece, and the variety of hues in the elongated wings could well serve a group pondering the direction of their ongoing discernment process.

Contemporary mosaics are made with small cubes of porcelain enamel, a silicate glass fired on metal, marble, glass and sometimes, mother-of-pearl. Mosaics absorb and reflect all the light that strikes them. In addition to light and color, rhythm is yet another characteristic of mosaics.

There are other possibilities for constructing mosaics that border on found art sculpture, but whose materials may be more accessible in your location. Mosaics have been made with fibers, with stones and with paper. One source on the techniques of making mosaics is *Making Mosaics: Designs, Techniques and Projects*, by Leslie Dierks.

The National Gallery of Art in Washington, D.C. houses the collection *Textiles from the Index of American Design* exhibit. Produced in America during the Eighteenth and Nineteenth Centuries by professional weavers as well as by workers in textile mills, some pieces in the display resemble fabric mosaics. Choice of color and placement of the fabrics give a sense of movement and rhythm as they do to enamel or glass mosaics.

Mosaics with Natural Stones, by Walter Lauppi, describes for beginners the types of stones and tools needed in making a stone mosaic as well as suggestions for planning and setting the artwork. As with textiles, the shape, grain and color of stones help suggest the style and form of a mosaic. Some artists prefer to work with alabaster, since it is available in a variety of colors.

A paper mosaic is similar to a paper sculpture, a quilting or a weaving, and may be created with a flexible weight of paper and a variety of colors. Libraries, museums and the World Wide Web are sources for examples that may spark your own creativity. There are also some helpful, inexpensive paperback books in the crafts section of bookstores. One such book is *Paper Making*, by Marion Elliot. In it the reader is shown how to make a paper leaf frieze, a marbeled bowl and a textured paper wallhanging using recycled paper and simple kitchen materials.

Guiseppe Bovina writes about the famous *Ravenna Mosaics* from the Fifth and Sixth Centuries, displayed in The Mausoleum of Galla

Placida near the Church of San Vitale in Ravenna, Italy: "The figures are more like visions than human beings since they are organized on rhythms resembling the verses of a psalm, giving them uniformity and cadence both in general appearance as well as in physiognomy, gestures and costumes. The indivisible elements of light, color and rhythm give the mosaics of Ravenna still another typical quality: the capacity of the broad surface of color to transform space and dematerialize the architectural structure, producing an intangible halo of atmosphere which varies with the change of natural light." [30]

The Walk Home, by Julian Schnabel (1984-1985) at the Pace Gallery in New York, is a vast mosaic of broken crockery, bronze and fiberglass painted and glued onto a wood support. The 9'3"x19'4" thickly impacted, jagged surface deflects the artists hand. It appears that the work was created by a random and automatic painting process. The mosaic-like texture is an amalgamation of media, bringing together painting, mosaic and low-relief sculpture.

I see in this work a wooded forest, a pond of water and glimpses of sunshine. I see a ground cover of leaves and some trash carelessly left behind. "What do you see?" What signs of life do you see?" "Are there signs of neglect in the scene?" "Are there signs of death, or impending death?"

Using this mosaic or another, what questions can you devise which address the human mosaic God's Spirit is creating during spiritual discernment? Some starter questions will be found when we explore the Movements of spiritual discernment in the following Chapters.

SCULPTURE

Kansas City has many outdoor public sculptures. In fact, on the fifty-five acres of The Plaza, there are fifty-five sculptures placed in varied sites. A favorite of mine is *Ruth*, sculpted of Carrare marble by Pasquale Romanelli. Ruth is depicted kneeling on one knee looking up and off to her right. When I become engaged in a process of spiritual discernment, the site of that sculpture might well become one of my

---

[30] Guiseppe Bovini. Ravenna Mosaics. Greenwich, CN: New York Graphic Society c. 1956 in Italy.

sacred spaces for ongoing prayer and reflection. I simply resonate with that sculpture. It centers and focuses my heart and thoughts.

The sculpture, *Pax Christi*, (the peace of Christ), is displayed at Saint John's Abbey, a Benedictine monastery in Collegeville, Minnesota. Christ, fully bearded, with sandals on his feet, is holding the book of the Gospels in his left hand. It is engraved with a cross at the center and with four circles in the corners symbolizing the four evangelists. With his right hand, Christ is pronouncing peace.

"How is the peace of Christ being summoned during this process of spiritual discernment?" "What aspects of the character of Jesus, as portrayed in one or more accounts of the four evangelists, are important to take onto oneself during this process of discernment?" "What commitment to evangelization is required which will show respect for the culture of the community affected by our eventual decision?"

Many of you will remember the International Peace Crane Project, the making of origami (paper) doves by school children and adults all over the world to promote world peace. Fabric origami doves have since been made, and detailed instructions, photos and diagrams for making them and other fabric origami subjects can now be found on the World Wide Web. Perhaps the group in discernment could create an Origami sculpture. Origami is defined as the Japanese art of folding paper into representational or decorative shapes.

The Servant Christ, a sculpture by Jimilu Mason, is placed in front of an inner-city clinic for the homeless, Christ House, in Washington, D.C. It is so striking that it immediately confronts anyone approaching the buildings' entrance. The sculpture is of a life-size man wearing jeans and a work shirt with the sleeves rolled up. He kneels on his left knee with his hands poised over a shallow basin. His face is turned upwards, looking into the eyes of anyone who stops long enough to ponder this figure. The sculpture presents for contemplation a model of servanthood embodied in the life and teachings of Jesus of Nazareth.

Many comments or questions stemming from gazing upon this sculpture can be used in spiritual discernment. Some particular themes around which to focus questions could be: care and neglect, the sharing of bread --"upon what are our eyes focused?"--, hunger and thirst, postures of servanthood, etc.

Art representing the crucifixion and the risen Christ is commonly seen, but a sculpture that attempts to present the moment of resurrection is rare. In a smaller-than-life sculpture, *Resurrection II*, by Paul T.

Granlund, of cast bronze, 1973, reproduced in *ARTS Advocate*, UCC Fellowship in the Arts, 12, no. 1, Winter, 1990, the figure of Christ is shown bent over, knees and head nearly touching, arms outstretched in a position of crucifixion. The figure is bound on three sides by slabs of the tomb, and on the fourth by the earth. Close examination reveals holes in the top and in the right side panel where the arm would have protruded when the panels were tightly closed around the body. The movement of Christ's body is not downward, but upward and out. The propelling tension in the legs emphasizes his surging strength as the lid of the tomb is thrown off. What a powerful reminder that the walls of death are not strong enough to prevail against the power of God!

As we journey through the Movements of spiritual discernment in the following Chapters, think about how the provocative image of this sculpture might be applied to some specific Movements, and to the lenten season, should you be meeting during this time in the church year.

Augustus Saint-Gaudens (1848-1907), an American sculptor who trained in France, used realism effectively in a number of his sculptures. However, for the design of a memorial monument of *Mrs. Henry Adams*, Saint-Gaudens chose "a classical mode of representation, which he modified freely. Of course he had no need to specify a particular character; he wanted to represent a generality outside of time and place. The resultant statue is that of a woman of majestic bearing sitting in mourning, her classically beautiful face partly shadowed by a sepulchural drapery that voluminously enfolds her body. The immobility of her form, set in an attitude of eternal viligance, is only slightly stirred by a natural, yet mysterious and exquisite gesture."[31]

This profound sculpture speaks to me of the posture of waiting-- what may seem like eternal vigilance--in spiritual discernment. The sculpture speaks to me of yet much more, but my wish is to have others interpret for themselves that "natural, yet mysterious and exquisite gesture."[32]

One of the most famous sculptures is Michaelangelo's masterpiece, *La Pieta*, depicting Mary holding the dead Christ after his body is taken down from the cross. Another is Michaelangelo's *David*. Another is Rodan's *The Thinker*. These too, and others, have much to

---

[31] Richard G. Tansey, Fred. S. Kleiner. Gardner's Art Through the Ages. Fort Worth, TX: Harcourt Brace College Publishers, 1996, pp 1010-1011.
[32] Ibid. p 1011.

offer discerners as they spend time gazing upon them. Note their stance, their apparent movement, their bulk, their height, their depth, their texture, their composition, their placement, etc.

There is yet another type of sculpture. Found Object Sculpture is made when artists adapt common, ordinary manufactured objects such as machinery parts, into their works. While living in San Francisco during the late 1960's and early 1970's, I witnessed the creation of much found object art along the shores of San Francisco Bay between Oakland and Berkeley. Every time I traveled that highway it seemed that there were new, larger and more intricate pieces. Today I muse on the possibilities for creating a found object sculpture during a process of spiritual discernment for the purpose of symbolizing the emerging decision within the dynamics of the Movements. Could a found object sculpture be created by your group? Note some suggestions in the following Chapters.

Or, do you have, or could you find a found object sculpture to share with the group in discernment? If you do this, let the sculpture speak for itself in the process. Do not force its symbolism on the group. Simply ask: "How does this sculpture speak to you about our process?" It may grow on the group or it may not. If it does have some significance, allow room for creative additions to the sculpture or to its base as spiritual discernment continues.

The Presbyterian Women (PCUSA) organization has a 1997 Birthday Offering poster by artist Kevin Darst that reflects the above concept. The background is wheat grass, symbolizing the bread of life that is supporting, surrounding and watching over the sculpture of a mother and child. Above their heads two small hands reach out as if they are extending grace toward them. The mother and child are obviously oppressed, yet the woman is very loving and comforting of her child. The oppressed nature of the figures and the tall wheat represent ministries to which the women are directing their funds this particular year. What found objects might the group in discernment add to their chosen sculpture?

Other artists such as Andy Goldsworthy of Scotland, does likewise with nature. He works with stones, wood and water. He is currently engaged in the *Sheepfolds* project that was begun in 1996 as part of the United Kingdom Year of the Visual Arts. His work is nothing short of physical poetry. The San Jose California Museum of Art gave Goldworthy his first show in an American museum in 1995, and it turned out to be one of the institution's most popular events in its history.

Perhaps the group or individuals within it could create a sculpture using elements of nature, or discover a poster or photograph of such a sculpture that has meaning for the group, i.e., "PIETA" (1955) by Fritz Eichenberg in *A Portfolio of Prints*. As spiritual discernment continues, you can expect whatever type of sculpture you choose to take on more and more significance for the group.

MUSIC

Edward Foley's book, *From Age To Age*, is a wonderful, fascinating, well illustrated and easily readable resource book on the history of art, architecture, music, vessels and books used in worship from the First Century up to the present day within an ecumenical context. It is probably one of my most often used reference books. Let me share with you some of Foley's research in the field of church music. I deem this pertinent information for discernmentarians.

Ambrose of Milan (d. 397), often called the Father of Western Hymnody, divided the texts of hymns into short stanzas, each one following the same pattern (number of lines, meter and rhyme scheme) as the previous stanza. This pattern has, as I'm sure you realize, been followed for centuries. It could even be true that early hymns may have been sung to well known secular tunes.

Around 1903, while composers of secular music explored new dimensions of rhythm, harmony and form, churches reverted back to music from the past. "Although artistic advances eventually influenced church music, it was not the composers of liturgical music who transformed Twentieth-Century worship music. It was, rather, the liturgical movement, which insisted that worship song was the people's song."[33]

In his discussion of ethnomusicology, Edward Foley writes that "another important trend in Twentieth Century music was an increased interest in folk music, in the music of non-Western cultures and in the role of music in culture...[generating] a new science called comparative

---

[33] Edward Foley, <u>From Age To Age</u>. Chicago, IL: Liturgy Training Publications, 1991, p 151.

musicology...Because music is integral to the rituals of many peoples, ethnomusicologists often study the ritual music of traditional societies."[34]

During the Christmas season, many church assemblies sing with gusto "Go Tell It On The Mountain", a song initially sung by African American slaves on the plantations. This song is part of the fiber of American culture, its use now transcending one nationality. Verse two addresses the journey of spiritual discernment: "When I was a seeker I sought both night and day; I ask the Lord to help me, And he shows me the way."[35]

Pastor, theologian and martyr Dietrich Bonhoeffer posed this question for himself: Why do Christians sing when they are together? He replied to himself: "The reason is, quite simply, because in singing together it is possible for them to speak and pray the same word at the same time; in other words, because here they can unite in the Word... It is the voice of the church that is heard in singing together. It is not you that sings, it is the church that is singing, and you, as a member of the church, may share in its song. Thus all singing together that is right must serve to widen our spiritual horizon, make us see our little company as a member of the great Christian church on earth, and help us willingly and gladly to join our singing, be it feeble or good, to the song of the church." [36]

In spiritual discernment, we must search together as the church , "to speak and pray the same word at the same time", and try to bring all the spiritual resources and gifts we have to the process. Music as symbolic language carries the power to connect us with our deepest selves, with our Creator God at the heart of the cosmos and the core of our being, and with the whole of creation. Drawing together body, mind, emotions and spirit in a unity of focus, music reveals and clarifies what is going on inside ourselves. It reveals us to ourselves.

Music in spiritual discernment needs to empower and facilitate our cultural diversity. It needs to speak to our oneness and to our uniqueness. It needs to respond to our varied and rich artistic traditions, and it needs to challenge us in our relationships with God and with each

---

[34] Ibid, p 153.

[35] Hugh Keyte, Andrew Parrott, eds., The New Oxford Book of Carols. New York, NY: Oxford University Press, 1972, p 573.

[36] Deitrich Bonhoeffer, Life Together. New York, NY: Harper and Row, 1954, p 59.

other. When music clothes a text, dimensions of feeling, meaning and intuition are unveiled that go beyond the text alone. Basic emotions and convictions then spill over in songs of praise, joy, lament, yearning and thanksgiving. You will find specific musical references and suggestions for their implementation on the following pages that highlight the Movements inherent within spiritual discernment.

The church has a rich tradition of Gregorian Chant. The church also has many versions of modern day chant. The music of the monks of Taize, France, an ecumenical community of brothers who are joined, especially in the summertime, by persons young and old from all around the world who are attracted to their spirituality as expressed in song, as well as the music of the Benedictine monks of Santo Domingo de Silos, are just a few of the contemporary resources available on CD's or cassette tapes. The monks of Taize's chants: "Veni Sancte Spiritus", "Nada Te Turbe"/Nothing Can Trouble", "Our Darkness/La Tenebre", and "Jesus, Remember Me", are all powerful repetitious, easy to sing a cappella chants which can be selected for their relevancy to the church's liturgical calendar and the matter at hand.

I've had the good fortune to attend concerts by The Anonymous 4. These four women combine musical, literary, and historical scholarship to create innovative concerts that interweave medieval chant and polyphony with poetry and narrative. They show delicate musicianship and possess hauntingly beautiful voices. They beguile an audience with their warmth of sound and obvious closeness of communication in performance. The Anonymous 4 perform concert series throughout the world, and they also record exclusively for harmonia mundi usa. Inclusion of some of their music as background meditation music, some appropriate for specific seasons of the church year, will add refreshing waters to a process of spiritual discernment.

St. Augustine is often quoted as the source of "singing is praying twice." By using God's gift of music, we are able to unite in the Word of God, joining our prayer to the prayer of the universal church.

The *Pachabel Canon in D Major*, by Johann Pachabel (1653-1706), provides a wonderful musical setting for spiritual discernment. Universally recognized, this piece of music may lead discerners into quiet sooner than an unfamiliar composition. In subsequent Chapters, I will suggest some musical compositions pertinent to specific Movements in discernment. We'll continue to discover how music can touch our hearts and souls.

But before we move on, let me name a few secular and very familiar songs we might use in spiritual discernment. From the musical *Godspell*, with music and lyrics by Stephen Schwartz, we have the following: "Prepare Ye the Way of the Lord", " Day by Day", "Bless the Lord", and "We Beseech Thee." From *Jesus Christ Superstar*, music by Andrew Lloyd Weber, lyrics by Tim Rice, there is "I Don't Know How to Love Him."

The wonderful hymn "Moved by the Gospel, Let us Move" seems to capture in poetic melody the call God gives discernmentarians to facilitate spiritual discernment.

"Moved by the Gospel, let us move
With every gift and art.
The image of creative love
Indwells each human heart.
The Maker calls creation good,

So let us now express
With sound and color, stone and wood,
The shape of holiness.

Let weavers form from broken strands
A tapestry of prayer.
Let artist paint with skillful hands
Their joy, lament, and care.
Then mime the story: Christ has come.
With rev'rence dance the word.
With flute and organ,
ching and drum
God's praise be ever heard.

O Spirit, breathe among us here;
Inspire the work we do.
May hands and voices, eye and ear
Attest to life made new.
In worship and in daily strife
Create among us still.
Great Artist, form our common life
According to your will.[37]

Persons who enter into a process of spiritual discernment can be likened to Schubert in the process of composing his *Unfinished*

---

[37] Ruth Dick, Ralph Vaughan Williams, <u>Moved by the Gospel, Let us Move</u>, <u>Gather Comprehensive</u>, Chicago, IL: GIA Publishers, 1994.

Symphony. The key has been established; the melody is in the process of being defined; the notes and spaces are in place, but may still take surprising twists; harmonies and descants are yet in developmental stages, but will continue to surface even after publication of the score.

DRAMA

During a January, 1997, School for Discernmentarians sponsored jointly by Worshipful-Work and The Upper Room, our process was aided in a very special way by one of the participants, Vernagaye Sullivan, a Methodist pastor from The Plains, Ohio. She presented a one-woman play entitled *Julian of Norwich*, written by J. Janda, an award-winning poet, a Jesuit priest, and a hospital chaplain in Denver, Colorado.

Vernagaye assumed the character of Julian, an English mystic, writer and spiritual guide born in 1342. Julian was an anchoress who lived a life of strict solitude, penance and prayer in a small cell attached to the Church of St. Edmund and St. Julian in Norwich, East Anglia. She studied, sewed clothing for the poor, and listened to those who came to her for spiritual guidance during the years of the One Hundred Years' War, three outbreaks of the Black Plague, the violent Peasants' Revolt and the Great Western Schism.

Vernagaye, in a very simple theater-in-the-round setting, led us deep into the character of Julian. Julian, near the age of thirty, received sixteen mystical visions regarding Christ crucified and his sorrowful mother, the incarnation, our redemption, sin, penance, and divine consolation. While creating a unique language for developing her mystical doctrines, Julian developed images of the Creator as father and mother, of Jesus as brother and savior, and of the Spirit as spouse.

Julian's vivid reflections during the one hour and twenty minute play were tempered with light-hearted musings on the glories of children playing in the street and on her simple delight in soft rainfalls. Likewise, Julian's childlike amusements over a mouse whom she fed in her cell were held alongside her intense worry over her sick friend, Marjery Kempe.

This play was an intense emotional experience for Verngaye and a profound experience for her audience. It helped all of us become more knowledgeable about Julian, our ancestor in faith, a person known centuries after her death (1420) for her goodness in the daily struggle with sin. In that struggle, Julian always found the ever-present divine mercy of God.

In your situation, what are the possibilities for including live drama in a spiritual discernment process? Are you, or is a discerner engaged in the process with you, involved in theater productions? Is there a play that would lend itself to the process currently being performed in the area? I encourage such research.

Is there a resource person/s in your congregation, someone who enjoys acting in drama, performing in skits, or who is a mime? Recently I was impressed with a televised performance of Cirque du Soleil, the internationally acclaimed French Canadian theatrical circus devoted solely to human performance. This high-spirited troupe performs high-caliber acrobatics, juggling, dance and mime. Entranced by their imaginative vision, I particularly enjoyed one segment wherein a mime led a volunteer from the audience in a mimed scenario. No words were exchanged; the volunteer simply responded to the motions of the mime. Could a story be told in this way during spiritual discernment? I think so.

While live drama is a preferred medium, is there a videotape of a drama that is particularly pertinent to the matter for spiritual discernment? You might peruse the nearest tape library or video store, noting the themes apparent in particular dramas. Remember that the drama, live or on tape, should be integral to the process of discernment, not extraneous to it. It should give food for thought to the participants in discernment, and some reflection questions for sharing should be prepared by the discernmentarian ahead of the viewing.

GLASS

Stained glass is glass that is colored by fusing colored metallic oxides onto the glass or by painting and baking transparent colors on the glass surface. Much that was previously written about paintings applies equally well to stained glass, but few human creations are capable of changing in intensity of color and depth with the addition of a ray of sunshine or a new cloud formation than a piece of stained glass. Very often artists relegate this medium solely to the explicitly pictorial. I believe stained glass formed as an abstraction can also be very beautiful and can say something to us that often words and pictures cannot.

I once toured a church where the interior had been renovated and a large space for classrooms and meetings had been added onto the original structure. I was enthralled by one meeting space where the congregation's council met. It has a large, round stained glass window depicting joined hands and a loaf of bread. What a wonderful visual art to contemplate during church meetings! Could you as discernmentarian challenge the group to develop a temporary, or permanent visual piece of art using a significant symbol? What could you design?

Little known outside the coterie of stained glass enthusiasts, Rowan LcCompte has created some of America's most beloved stained glass windows: *The Creation* rose window in the Episcopal Washington National Cathedral, an awe-inspiring fifteen feet wide by 30 feet tall window that stands amidst forty-four additional LcCompte windows designed and installed during the past fifty-six years; a window in the Governor's Chamber of the New York State Capitol; a window in the chapel of Princeton University; a window in St. Matthew's Episcopal Cathedral in Laramie, Wyoming, and five stained glass windows for the magnificent 1913 House of Hope Presbyterian Church in St. Paul, Minnesota. Given blank canvases and instructions to inspire viewers, LeCompte was at the same time offered opportunities to bring the sacredness of life into his viewers' consciousness. Could not a group in spiritual discernment do the same via this medium?

One informative and inexpensive resource on basic materials and basic techniques is *Stained Glass, Contemporary Crafts*, by Marc Gerstein. The paperback book is beautifully illustrated and it is rather easy for beginners to follow.

A stained glass candleholder can be used as a focal point for dialogue and worship. These are available in many specialty stores and from mail order catalogues. A good source for the latter is Terry's Village, P.O. Box 2309, Omaha, NE 68103-2309. A comparable and economical substitute is a hand-blown glass oil lamp. Different effects may be created by using clear or colored oils.

One can find Seeded Glass candlestick holders in antique shops and museums under the name "Waldglas." Essentially unchanged since the Fifteenth Century, the European Waldglas (German for "forest glass") technique produces air bubbles magically trapped in glass. Glassblowers add sodium powder at even intervals to create glass that is consistently seeded. A candle the color of the liturgical season placed in a seeded glass hurricane lamp or topping a 4"-5" in diameter round candleholder will add rich color and the ambiance of a prism to the setting for spiritual discernment.

The Metropolitan Museum of Art in New York City offers catalogues and retail shops across the country from which beautiful art pieces designed from objects in the Museum's collection can be purchased. Some examples of glass artwork are the following: *Christmas Star*, a 4 ¼ x 6½ card of a stained glass panel from a German Nativity scene (1445); *Mackintosh Poster*, a 19" x 32 ½" leaded-glass splashboard by Charles Rennie Mackintosh (Scottish: 1868-1928) showing two Menorah's (seven-branched candelabrum of the Jewish Temple symbolizing the seven days of Creation); and two stained glass panels created by the Tiffany Studios early in this century, *Magnolia And Irises*, height 13", and *Dogwood*, height 16 ¼." These small scale reproductions are made of transparent enamels silk-screened and then fired onto hand-rolled glass.

When traveling in Italy, a friend of mine purchased a small pewter cross with gold inlaid stained glass outlining the shape of the cross as a gift. In the center of the pewter cross is a stained glass figure of the risen Jesus, arms held high, in white and green colored glass. Perhaps you have access to a similar art piece.

Peonies Blowing in the Wind, a leaded glass window 56 ½" x 26 ½", by John LaFarge, circa 1889, is beautifully and singularly displayed in the Nelson Gallery in Kansas City, Missouri. Framed with a glass border imitating silk on a Japanese scroll (kakemono), the window depicts red and blue windswept peonies against a dark background with a few serrated clouds and a bit of landscape. The window appears to be full of movement and energy. As is true for many paintings, this glass window is available for purchase from a poster series (Lithographic Philanthropic Poster Series) and in hardcover books dedicated to LaFarge's numerous works. At least three versions of *Peonies Blowing in the Wind* are now in public collections. The version at the Seattle Art Museum was retained by the artist throughout his life (1835-1910).

Is there someone in the group who works with stained glass? Could a special stained glass creation be made as part of the group's spiritual discernment? New York's Metropolitan Museum of Art publishes a book called *Fun With Stained Glass*, by Mary B. Shepard and Fifi Weinert. If working with real glass isn't a practical consideration for a group is spiritual discernment, this book contains eight Museum designs on acetate sheets to color with translucent paints. The book also includes a paintbrush and mixing tray. The artistry of working with or observing the creation of a stained glass piece might well assist a group's process.

The ability of glass to reflect, retract, attract or hold light makes discernment a good setting for it, day or night, and a piece of glass on a glass table makes it even more reflective. Glass pieces of art, created in literally countless ways for diverse looks, may be carved, layered, threaded or slumped, a process in which liquid glass is placed over a mold to produce a final shape. Toots Zynsky, whose work is in New York's Museum of Modern Art and is available at the Elliott Brown Gallery in Seattle, heats thousands of colored glass threads and fuses them together, pulling them into sculptural bowl shapes that undulate as though they are being blown by the wind. This process allows Zynsky to work like a sculptor and a painter. His work, and all glass art, is open to individual interpretation by each and every beholder. In summary, we are allowed to have a conversation and a relationship with the glass work of art.

END NOTES

Discernmentarians need not be intent on using specific rituals and specific art mediums to help persons arrive at tidy conclusions. They need to be able to improvise, finding great joy in weaving a variety of artistic resources into the Movements in spiritual discernment.

Discernmentarians, like artists, use many tools to accomplish their work. Yet, when all these tools have been used, and the specific work of art is completed, the artistic creation has really just begun. The mystery inherent in each work of art, or each decision by spiritual discernment, continues.

I am reminded in this reflection of what one pianist said after being praised for how well he handled the notes: *Anyone can handle the notes. But the spaces between the notes. That is the art.* Discernmentarians live in that paradox.

Chapter Three

Weaving Ritual & The Arts
Throughout The Movements Of
Framing -- Grounding -- Shedding -- Rooting

How can a discernmentarian weave ritual and the arts into each movement in spiritual discernment? I certainly cannot answer that question completely, but I may be able to point to some particularly helpful ways from my own personal experience as a discernmentarian.

Many of the prophetic texts in our Advent liturgies spell our God's yearning for us. Let me cite just two examples from Isaiah. In Isaiah 2:3-5 we read: "Many peoples shall come and say, 'Come, let us go up to the mountain of the Lord, to the house of the God of Jacob; that he may teach us his ways and that we may walk in his path's. For out of Zion shall go forth instruction, and the word of the Lord from Jerusalem. He shall judge between the nations, and shall arbitrate for many peoples; they shall beat their swords into plowshares, and their spears into pruning hooks; nation shall not lift up sword against nation, neither shall they learn war any more." In Isaiah 11:6 we read: "The wolf shall live with the lamb, the leopard shall lie down with the kid, the calf and the lion and the fatling together, and a little child shall lead them."

Wouldn't you agree with me that in contemporary times it is God's yearning that people in the Middle East and other troubled areas of our world be able to share the same piece of land and sit at the same dinner tables? Wouldn't you agree with me that it is a portion of God's yearning that Martin Luther King articulated for us in 1963 in his *I Have a Dream* speech: "I have a dream that one day this nation will rise up and live out the true meaning of its creed: "We hold these truths to be self-evident, that all men are created equal. I have a dream that one day on the red hills of Georgia the sons of former slaves and the sons of former slave-owners will be able to sit down together at the table of brotherhood. I have a dream that my four little children will one day live in a nation where they will not be judged by the color of their skin but by the content of their character."[38]

---

[38] Martin Luther King. I Have A Dream. September, 1963.

Martin Luther King's dream illustrates the importance of having not only a vision, but a language that can inspire persons to draw upon resources from the rich potential of their imaginations and move beyond the limiting facts of past and present experiences. Believing in our dynamic, active God who is always present in the midst of our circumstances, let us move in faith to learn, grow and change. This is part of the challenge of engaging in spiritual discernment: to dream as God dreams. Let's not dream in a familiar "planning" mode, but reach for God's vision and yearning out of our rootedness as a people of God.

How, then, can a discernmentarian facilitate imperative and sometimes difficult matters within the framework of spirituality? There is no clear, cookie-cutter, unequivocal formula for discerning God's will or yearning, but Charles M. Olsen and Danny E. Morris's book, *Discerning God's Will Together: A Spiritual Practice for the Church*, names and explains the Movements inherent in the practice of spiritual discernment. These Movements are fluid in any discernment process by which we come to know God's yearning, or God's dream, for us. These Movements, helpful to a discernmentarian because they have been named, are not processed in the sequential, linear sequence that follows. The Movements begin, however, with *Framing* a matter for discernment, and conclude with the *Resting* Movement. The Movements are:

FRAMING - Selecting The Subject For Discernment;
GROUNDING - Choosing A Guiding Principle;
SHEDDING - Coming To Indifference About The Outcome;
ROOTING - In Biblical Tradition;
LISTENING - To The Voices Needing To Be Heard;
EXPLORING - All Possible Options;
IMPROVING - Each One Of The Options;
WEIGHING - The Integrity Of Each Option;
CLOSING - Choosing The Most Viable Option.
RESTING - Taking The Test Of The Heart.

In *Discerning God's Will Together, A Spiritual Practice for the Church*, Olsen and Morris present three visual images with which to look at these Movements (pages 67-69): a reflection pool with ten stepping stones, a spiral orbiting around a magnetic core (God's will), and a field of grain (the selecting and planting of seed, cultivating the plants and

57

harvesting the yield). I will use the latter image as we look at each Movement and how it gives occasion to incorporate ritual and the arts. Rituals and the arts can be incorporated into the process of spiritual discernment if there are no major obstacles to overcome, as well as assist an individual or the group to become "unstuck" if the situation warrants it. The use of ritual and the arts in spiritual discernment is meant to enhance and deepen the experience of coming to discover—or uncover-- God's yearning, or God's dream.

The following content then, is keyed to the Olsen/Morris book *Discerning God's Will Together: A Spiritual Practice for the Church*, in which these ten Movements are explained in extensive detail.

SELECTING THE SEED
"A farmer carefully selects the seed. The right seed needs to be selected to fit the climate and soil conditions."[39]

FRAMING - The group or individual selects the matter for spiritual discernment. The "heart of the matter" is identified. The focus is narrow enough for group reflection. The ultimate question is "God, is this your yearning?"

The matter for spiritual discernment should obviously be a serious one. Those entering into spiritual discernment are seeking to receive divine guidance on the matter by praying, contemplating, studying and dialoguing about the matter over a period of time.

Nelson Mandela, in his inaugural address to the people of South Africa, a people who have paid dearly to live out their yearning for release from bondage, used the following quote from Marianne Williamson. I believe it also offers us some wisdom for processing the *Framing* Movement:

---

[39] Olsen, Charles M. and Danny E. Morris. Discerning God's Will Together: A Spiritual Practice for the Church. Washington, D.C.: The Alban Institute; Nashville, TN: The Upper Room, 1997, p 69.

"OUR DEEPEST FEAR
IS NOT THAT WE ARE INADEQUATE
OUR DEEPEST FEAR IS THAT
WE ARE POWERFUL BEYOND MEASURE.

IT IS OUR LIGHT AND NOT OUR DARKNESS
THAT FRIGHTENS US.
WE ASK OURSELVES, 'WHO AM I TO BE
BRILLIANT, GORGEOUS, TALENTED AND
FABULOUS?'
ACTUALLY WHO ARE YOU NOT TO BE?
YOUR PLAYING SMALL DOESN'T SERVE THE
WORLD.

THERE'S NOTHING ENLIGHTENED ABOUT
SHRINKING
SO THAT OTHER PEOPLE WON'T FEEL INSECURE
AROUND YOU.
WE ARE BORN TO MAKE MANIFEST
THE GLORY OF GOD THAT IS WITHIN US.
IT IS NOT JUST IN SOME OF US
IT IS IN EVERYONE.

AND AS WE LET OUR OWN LIGHT SHINE,
WE UNCONSCIOUSLY GIVE OTHER PEOPLE
PERMISSION TO DO THE SAME.
AS WE ARE LIBERATED FROM OUR FEAR,
OUR PRESENCE AUTOMATICALLY LIBERATES
OTHERS. [40]

"From where will the framed question come?" "What events have/are leading up to the asking of this framed question?" "Am I/are we entering into this process as a humble, lovable child of God wanting to "make manifest" God's yearning in this matter?" Discernmentarians pay attention to the energy present in the descriptions and in the quiet.

---

[40] Marianne Williamson. <u>A Return to Love</u>. New York, NY: Harpercollins, 1992, p 24.

"What are the feelings that are conveyed, and what meanings do they embody?"

Icons of modern saints such as those saluted in *A Passion for Life:Fragments of the Face of God*, written by Joan Chittister with artwork by Robert Lentz, suggests to me the possibility of participants in spiritual discernment bringing their own "icons", which may be a photograph or an article of any type to help tell their story and frame it. Icons, being special kinds of images, are companions on a journey. And as we select life companions carefully, we need to be careful in choosing an icon to help us tell the unfolding story of our discernment.

The icon, as well as participants in the discernment group, may encourage, nudge or challenge the story and its *Framing*. For example, if the matter for spiritual discernment deals with a woman's role in the church, and if the group chooses the *Mary Magdalene* icon by Robert Lentz to help frame the matter, be assured that this image will provide insights regarding the dignity of women in the church. The discernmentarian may ask questions such as these of the gazers: "What do you see?" "What do you notice about the position and movements of her physical features?" "What significance is there in the colors?", etc., and follow up on the reflections and insights of the participants. It would then be well to periodically come back to this icon for further contemplation and reflection.

Art that is compelling and poignant often comes from artists whose lives are alienated and marginated, or artists whose sensitivity to injustices causes them to live and minister among those whose lives are so. By whatever medium of expression, the reality of the situation is captured. It is then that beholders can accept the Spirit of God's invitation to conjure up reconfigurations of that reality not yet available in the circumstance of the situation. Is there a painting that contains elements of the issue to be framed? (Some possibilities were cited in Chapter Two.) Would a dialogue about the elements in the art piece help to frame the matter for spiritual discernment?

Participants in conferences on spiritual discernment affirm the fact that *Framing* takes time, and that it is often more difficult than expected. *Framing* takes careful listening because one idea leads to the creation of another. *Framing* is a time of narrowing and refining many thoughts and feelings into a simple, focused statement.

At the end of Christopher Fry's play *A Sleep of Prisoners*, the character of Joe Meadows speaks these lines: [for an inclusive pronoun, insert "we" for "men"]

> *"The human heart can go to the lengths of God.*
> *Dark and cold we may be, but this*
> *Is no winter now. The frozen misery*
> *Of centuries breaks, cracks, begins to move,*
> *The thunder is the thunder of the floes,*
> *The thaw, the flood, the upstart Spring.*
> *Thank God our time is now when wrong*
> *Comes up to face us everywhere,*
> *Never to leave us till we take*
> *The longest stride of soul men ever took.*
> *Affairs are now soul size.*
> *The enterprise*
> *Is exploration into God."*[41]

A matter for spiritual discernment is "soul size." The task in the *Framing* movement is to state the heart of the matter as succinctly as possible.

Anne Quigley wrote the text and tune for "There Is A Longing." The refrain is: "There is a longing in our hearts, O Lord, for you to reveal yourself to us...There is a longing in our hearts for love we only find in you, our God."[42] This refrain musically frames a process of spiritual discernment. In this *Framing* movement, we seek a vision and an action outcome to be developed prayerfully and lovingly over time, and on which God's Spirit rests, giving spiritual energy for the transformational process that lies ahead.

David Wilcox sings "Hold It Up To The Light", one of his folk compositions, on a CD entitled *Big Horizon* available in music stores and from A&M Records, Inc., P.O. Box 118, Hayward, California. This guitar rendition reflects upon the process of letting "light" into the process of making a personal decision. The melody is catching and haunting at the same time. This piece could be introduced during the

---

[41] Christopher Fry, <u>A Sleep of Prisoners</u>. New York, NY: Oxford University Press, 1951, pp 47-48.

[42] Anne Quiley, <u>There Is A Longing</u>, Portland, OR: Oregon Catholic Press, 1997 Music Issue.

Framing movement and experienced again as the discernment process continues.

Oliver Wendell Holmes, Jr.'s words give us impetus for *Framing*: "I find the great thing in this world is not so much where we stand, as in what direction we are moving."[43] I personally always find great strength in this prayer of St. Augustine: "O God, our hearts are made for thee, and they shall be restless until they rest in thee."[44] My spirit is restless until God's yearning has come to light.

Here's another artistic possibility to use while *Framing* a question for discernment: create a piece of art that captures and expresses the framed issue. A discernmentarian could suggest the art medium or merely provide materials from which to choose. The artistic creation will serve as a test of clarity about the framed question as well as an ongoing symbol to accompany persons in the process of discernment. If the group is large in number, dyads or triads could present the initial piece. Then invite others to add to it until the group is satisfied with the framed question.

Gourds are members of the squash family and when harvested they dry to hard, thick, woody shells. Known as the pottery of the plant world, they can be fashioned into useful and decorative objects. Some exquisitely painted gourds by the artist BRECKENRIDGE are displayed and for sale at the Northwest Art Studio at Sea-Tac Airport in Washington State. These gourds have been pyrographed with a heated tool and colored with dyes and inks. Kept out of direct sunlight, the fine inks and dyes retain their vibrant colors. The gourds can be safely used for dried flowers or simply enjoyed for their esthetic value.

The group in discernment may begin to decorate a large gourd during this *Framing* movement. The painting or inking may be done by one individual artist in response to suggestions by the whole group, or by everyone in the group over the period of time they are together. The artwork may be of realistic images, symbols and/or colors that reflect the group's life together. During the *Closing* movement in spiritual discernment the group may choose to fill the gourd with a plant or flower arrangement, or a different symbol. Group members could also choose to fill the inside of the gourd at various times throughout the discernment

---

[43] Oliver Wendell Holmes. The Autocrat of the Breakfast Table. 1891, p 93.

[44] Thelma Hall. Too Deep For Words. Rediscovering Lectio Divina. Mahwah, NJ: Paulist Press, 1998, p 42.

process.

I had an opportunity to observe Tibetian monks construct a mandala over a period of one week at the Nelson Gallery in Kansas City. Mandalas are circular designs arranged in layers radiating from the center. Mandalas designed by the Tibetian monks in the form of sand paintings are rich in symbolism. The slow, meticulous movement of creating the mandala leads the monks into a prayerful state by emptying their minds of other thoughts and centering them totally in the present moment.

Now, I'm not suggesting that a discernment group necessarily takes on the construction of a sand mandala. However the concept of mandala construction may be utilized in this *Framing* movement via photographs, small found objects such as pebbles or shells, even an illustrated paper chain which could change shapes, colors or sizes.

While engaged in the *Framing* movement, create the frame for a weaving that will eventually symbolize the persons and happenings throughout the Movements. I have used large embroidery hoops as a frame for a table group, smaller hoops for individual design. Cloth, paper, yarn, sticks--any material can be used for the weaving. As discernment continues, beads or other available found objects may be added to the weaving.

A weaving ritual to accompany prayer during this *Framing* Movement goes like this: with everyone sitting in a circle holding different colored rolls of crepe paper, the participants begin tossing their rolls to each other, forming a web that weaves around them and weaves them together. This action may be prefaced and accompanied by prayers of one's choosing, and/or include the following poem entitled "Indian Tapestry":

> "When I go up to the HOUSE OF THE OLD WEAVER
> I watch in admiration
> at what comes from her mind:
> a thousand designs being created
> and not a single model from which to copy
> the marvelous cloth
> with which she will dress the companion of the True
> and Faithful
> One.

63

Men always ask me
to give the name of the label,
to specify the maker of the design.
But the Weaver cannot be pinned down
by designs,
nor patterns.
All of her weavings are originals,
there are no repeated patterns.
Her mind is beyond
all foresight.
Her able hands do not accept patterns or models.
Whatever comes forth, comes forth,
but she who is will make it.

The colors of her threads
are firm: blood,
sweat,
perseverance,
tears,
struggle,
and hope.
Colors that do not fade
with time.

The children of the children
of our children
will recognize the seal
of the Old Weaver.
Maybe then
it will receive a name.
But as a model, it can never again be repeated.

Each morning I have seen how her fingers choose the
threads
one by one.

Her loom makes no noise and men give it no importance.
None-the-less, the design that emerges from Her Mind
hour after hour will appear in the threads of many
colors,
in figures and symbols which no one, ever again,
will be able to erase or un-do. [45]

In spiritual discernment there is no model to copy, but there is the yearning of God's Spirit to be found through prayer and perseverance in the process. Returning to this poem during future Movements may provide more than ample content for theological reflection on the process and the experience.

In this initial Movement, once the question for discernment has been framed, the follow-up question is: "God, is this your yearning?" The answer is to be found in the remainder of the process.

Let's now go further and deeper into the Movements of spiritual discernment. These next three Movements: *Grounding, Shedding,* and *Rooting* are captured under the heading *Planting The Seed.* Again, picture these Movements happening in an open and dynamic process, not necessarily as linear as this outline suggests.

PLANTING THE SEED

"A farmer prepares the soil and plants the seed. The good soil which is loose, rather than rocky and hard-packed, gives the seed a chance to grow. The seed is grounded in the soil of a guiding principle for our process of discernment.
The seed will die—that is, give itself up for the initial growth of the plant. In like manner, in discernment we are invited to shed, or give up, or come to indifference to anything but God's will. ... In discernment we root the process in tradition—both the ancient biblical tradition and the ongoing traditions and stories of the community of faith." [46]

---

[45] Julia Esquivel. Threatened With Resurrection. Elgin, IL: Brethren Press, 1982, p 56.
[46] Olsen, Charles M. and Danny E. Morris. Discerning God's Will Together: A Spiritual Practice for the Church. Washington, D.C.: The Alban Institute; Nashville, TN: The Upper Room, 1997, p 69.

GROUNDING - A Guiding Principle is selected. This Guiding Principle is informed by the values, beliefs and purpose of the discerning community. Attempt to ground the framed question in the spirituality of your Christian heritage.

Early photographs of Egypt and the American West are revelations of our pre-Twentieth Century lands and cultures, some picturesque and some revealing terrifying aspects of nature. Some current day photographers present "before" and "after" photographs of our national parks, laying bare the ecological damage that is being done to our surroundings. We are able to observe in texture or shape the continuing effects of weather and human encroachment on a particular piece of this earth.

The Guiding Principle in spiritual discernment is like a still photograph. It is something known very well. It is at once formative and familiar. It is as specific as possible. It tests the boundaries of what means to be prayerfully discerning. It gets to the heart of the matter. It ties persons to their common roots and to each other.

Suppose I was presently engaged in a process of spiritual discernment regarding a new opportunity for ministry. Aspects of a Guiding Principle could be taken from a statement from the Constitutions of my religious congregation: "...called to live in any part of the world where there is promise of furthering the mission of Jesus through works of education, justice and peace."[47] This needs to be carefully considered in my prayerful discernment, but a more specific Guiding Principle would be helpful to the process. So, I might be drawn to state the Guiding Principle as: "I will minister anywhere in the world where my gifts will further the mission of Jesus through education *in an ecumenical arena*." In this statement I have narrowed my focus to an ecumenical arena, but also tapped into the many still photographs of congregational members educating in a wide variety of ways since the mid 1800's.

The Irish have a word which speaks to me of *Grounding*. It is Grieshog. Gaelic speakers tell us it is the process of burying warm coals in ashes at night in order to preserve the fire for the cold morning to come. Instead of cleaning out the cold hearth, they preserve yesterday's

---

[47] Sisters of Charity, BVM. Constitutions. Dubuque, IA: Sisters of Charity, BVM, 1989, p 10.

glowing coals under beds of ash overnight in order to have a fast-starting new fire the next day. Different parts of the country have their own chants and blessings which are recited as the "smooring" of the fire is carried out, to ask protection for the house, the hearth and the people within it. The process is an extremely important one, because if the coals go out, a whole new fire must be built and lit when morning comes. This is an exercise that takes precious time and slows the more important work of the new day. It is a holy process, this *Grounding*, this preserving purpose, energy, warmth, and light as well as darkness.

A Guiding Principle could be "God's will, nothing else," but it is best to come up with a foundational principle that reflects the individual or group's life, is time-honored, and touches into the charism and values of those involved in the process of spiritual discernment.

A charism is a particular gift, flowing from a call by God, and given to individuals or a group for the good of the church. Catholic men's and women's religious congregations often speak of their particular charisms. Some congregations were founded for the work of education. They may have begun by building elementary and secondary schools and colleges. Yet today they are living out their charism of education also as directors of religious education, pastoral care workers and as pastoral administrators of parishes, to name but a few educational ministries. Is your group (or an individual) in discernment able to articulate and reflect on its charism? What leading questions need to be asked?

Experience tells us that a photograph keeps on showing us something new in the landscape. So does the Guiding Principle. In spiritual discernment we keep coming back to it as a reference point, and use it to keep uncovering something God's yearning knows only so well. That is why much care needs to be given to the formulation of the Guiding Principle. If there is difficulty in deciding on the Guiding Principle, move along in the process but return to this "stepping stone" in the reflection pond until a Guiding Principle is named.

A discernmentarian might ask individuals to attempt to describe the Guiding Principle in feeling words ("I feel the need for warm arms around my shoulders"). One could lead a reflection on the symbolism of the various images as they surface, and use them for spontaneous prayer, or for an extended prayer until the next session. Members of the group may wish to draw or doodle their symbols. Notice what is lifegiving and what is broken in the symbols. Ask: "What potential is there for newness and healing?" Perhaps the symbols will enable the prayer to go deeper within this *Grounding* Movement.

In the course of this *Grounding* Movement, it would be appropriate and certainly applicable to engage in planting flower or vegetable seeds in small pots or outdoors. Let these actions also be predominant images for prayer. The prayer could include a reading of John 15:1-17, the vine and the branches, followed by silence and by some time to reflect and share on the following question: "What meaning does being attached to the vine have for you?"

The following Guided Imagery exercise might follow a prayerful reading of John 15:1-17.

"Invite participants to close their eyes and call to mind a special plant they've nourished. *Remind the members that the growth of that plant required watering, proper lighting, warm or cool air, pruning on occasion...*

Invite them to move from thinking about a specific plant to imaging themselves as a branch—connected to the true vine. *Following are some questions you might use (pausing between them) to help persons image themselves:*

Is your branch green and ripe, ready to blossom?

Are you sturdy, healthy, somewhat gnarled and rough?

Are you young, delicate, needing older branches to show you how to blow in the wind?

Are you frail, needing more nurturing, afraid of the elements?

Are you grateful for the sturdy vine to which you're attached?

After a sufficient amount of time, invite the members to slowly open their eyes and enter into the group once again. [48]

After some sharing, conclude by praying from Isaiah 61:

I rejoice heartily in Yahweh, for I, We, have been clothed with a robe of salvation and wrapped in a mantle of justice. As the earth brings forth its plants,

---

[48] Morseth, Ellen. New Board/Council Member Orientation. Kansas City, MO: WORSHIPFUL-WORK: Center for Transforming Religious Leadership, 1996, p 6.

and a garden makes its growth spring up, so will God make justice and praise spring up before the nations. Amen.

Centering music, soft instrumental music on cassette tape or CD, might be used as the group is in the process of grounding themselves in the values, beliefs and purpose of their discerning community. *Earth Rhythms* blends sounds from nature with musical themes. The sounds of synthesizers, harps, harmonicas, acoustic guitars and percussion instruments are woven with the sounds of falling rain, babbling brooks and animal calls for "Stars Over the Canyon", "The Hills of Ireland", "African Plains", and "Glacier Point." *Shadows* is another centering tape with soft, soothing sounds. One of my favorite centering tapes is *The Fairy Ring.* It uses piano and synthesized strings and the melodies are calming and unobtrusive for private reflection. Humming along, if the tune is familiar or easily repetitive, can also be initiated by anyone.

Perhaps someone in the group is a composer and has his/her music on tape, or would play it for the group on an instrument. This is quite appropriate and would add to that person's sense of contributing a special gift to the esprit of the group.

Sometimes it is difficult for a group, or some discerners in a group, to refrain from entering into a planning mode throughout the Movements of spiritual discernment. When this happens, it often begins to surface during this *Grounding* Movement. Our secular cultures have so drawn us into assimilating managerial modes of operation that we need to call attention to their presence as they surface. If an individual is unaware of it happening, others in the group might well be helpful in providing this gatekeeping service.

> *SHEDDING* – entails coming to a personal and group stance of indifference to the outcome of the process. Let's give this a positive spin: I/We want to enter openly and honestly into prayerful reflection on our framed question and our Guiding Principle. I/We will make every effort to be honest in sharing, genuinely listen, and respond with empathy to anyone of us who comes to indifference in a difficult manner.

Ignatius' Rule 1.1 in his *Rules for Discernment* is that one should know one's weaknesses. We all have strengths and weaknesses and we exhibit them each day. The Movement of *Shedding* provides us an "out", a reason to intentionally state for our own good and for the benefit of others, our weaknesses in this situation, or our limitations. It gives us an opportunity to confess our failings and to be prayed for in a communal setting. *Shedding,* or letting go of something, is like being given the midway gift of a twelve-step program: the chance to lay before ourselves, and our friends in God, our failings and our yearning for healing. What an opportunity! Haven't we all said "life is too short for..."? This Movement brings an opportunity to bring those words to life.

During times of transition, we often are vulnerable and feel as if we are in danger of losing something important. Like animals that have outgrown their old skins and must shed what no longer fits, we feel exposed, soft, unprotected. The old skin, or that previous way of being, was at least warm and familiar to us. The new is often frightening and unfamiliar.

During the *Shedding* Movement, individuals name their attachments, their neediness, and what they find difficult to let go. Then they attempt to come to true indifference about them, seeking God's true yearning, not their own. The experience of doing this is often bittersweet. To admit first to oneself, then to the group in spiritual discernment, one's greediness about a desired outcome, or one's struggle with anger or jealousy about a particular situation, is a painful experience. Yet we know from scholarly research on the stages of death and dying that feelings and expressions of guilt and grief can, in God's good time, be transformed into true consolation and hope.

When we engage in *Shedding* our attachments during spiritual discernment we are performing a ritual of cleansing ourselves of that which is undesirable for our personal and group integrity. We are admitting our shadow side. We are attempting to burn out our impurities, smooth out our rough spots, acknowledge that within us which is in need of change. We are asking: "What limits me/us from being totally open to wherever God's Spirit leads?"

Other, more specific questions may need to be asked: "Where am I/we too narrow-minded?" "Am I inhibiting new possibilities?" "What in myself do I usually deny, and am I doing this again?" "What next step can we take to let go of _____?" "What am I clinging to?" "What is holding me/us captive?" "What is the prayer that I bring to this group and to God?"

A poem written by Joyce Rupp is one the group might recite during the *Shedding* Movement:

> *"something unnamed*
> *is being called forth*
> *in the depths*
>
> > *it has the familiar sound*
> > *of an Abraham*
> > *and the quiet certainty*
> > *of a sunrise*
> *it has the movement*
> *of geese surging*
> *past a season*
>
> > *of trees surrendering*
> > *to another snowfall*
> > *or another leafing*
>
> *something unnamed*
> *keeps calling*
>
> > *beckoning*
> > *rooting*
> > *growing*

something unnamed
asks for surrender

vulnerability
given-over-ness
abandonment
powerlessness

ah yes
the truth takes time
to be named
and even more time
to be accepted"[49]

Shedding requires a capacity to risk, to break old ties, to venture forth into a new and perhaps uncomfortable or unfamiliar order of things. We are challenged in this Movement to articulate our need to cut the tethers by which we have so ingeniously anchored ourselves. The apostle Paul speaks to us of a creation still waiting with "eager longing...to be set free from its bondage to decay and to obtain the glorious liberty of the children of God." (Romans 8:18-21) Through our attempts at *Shedding*, we give expression to God's abundant mercy and we image the redemptive God whose face is immutably turned to us in love.

Should an individual or an entire group reach what seems to be an impasse during this Movement, a discernmentarian may find a resource in the music of a particular culture to help the group give expression to its predicament.

Liberation music is created by the diaspora of various nations. It addresses the hurts of people and their desire for a better future. It reflects the mighty struggle to let attachments go in order to become free. Liberation music such as "Jou a Riva, The Day Will Come", which affirms Haiti's establishment as the first free Black nation in the Western Hemisphere, speaks loudly of *Shedding* or letting go, then grasping what is really God's yearning, true and essential. Invite the group to sing such

---

[49] Joyce Rupp. Fresh Bread and Other Gifts of Spiritual Nourishment. Notre Dame, IN: Ave Maria Press, 1988, p 134.

music a cappella, or play a tape and invite the group to join in the refrain. Add planned or spontaneous movements with hands/bodies as a group or solo expression.

Lamenting is a form of prayer in which the speaker exclaims and mourns about his or her need or misfortune and petitions God for assistance and deliverance. About one-third of the psalms are prayers of lamentation, some personal, some collective or uttered in the name of the community. Psalm 12, for example, could be incorporated into a time of prayer in which individuals and/or the group would petition God for deliverance from that which is difficult to shed. A symbol for this prayer is fire. The ideal environment for this prayer would include a working fireplace and comfortable chairs. If that is not feasible, a candle could be used as in the following description.

Following a Call to Prayer, the discernmentarian lights a candle and says: "Fire lends itself, serving our life." Then she/he turns to the next person and gives her/him the candlelight. The refrain is repeated by each person as they hold the candle. The candle is then placed in the center of the group, and someone prayerfully reads this poem by Elsa Gidlow entitled *Chains of Fire*:

"Each dawn, kneeling before my hearth
Placing stick, crossing stick
On dry eucalyptus bark
Now the larger boughs, the log
(With thanks to the tree for its life)
Touching the match, waiting for creeping flame,
I know myself linked by chains of fires
To every woman who has kept a hearth.

In the resinous smoke
I smell hut and castle and cave,
Mansion and hovel,
See in the shifting flame my mother
And grandmothers out over the world
Time through, back to the paleolithic
In rock shelters where flint struck first sparks
(Sparks aeons later alive on my hearth).
I see mothers, grandmothers back to beginnings,
Huddled beside holes in the earth

73

Of iglu, tipi, cabin,
Guarding the magic no other being has learned.
Awed, reverent, before the sacred fire
Shared live coals with the tribe.
For no one owns or can own fire,
It lends itself.
Every hearth-keeper has known this.
Hearth-less, lighting one candle in the dark
We know it today.
Fire lends itself.
Serving our life.[50]

After a few moments of silence following the reading, ask each person to name words or phrases that struck them. You may choose to follow up on any comments made, or lead a reflection on the awe and reverence for the sacredness of each persons' struggle to let go during times of *Shedding.* The point may be made that there will undoubtedly be times of further *Shedding* as our best intentions sometimes take more than one attempt at *Shedding* to really become a true part of us.

There is an icon entitled *Captive Daughter of Zion,* written by Robert Lentz in 1988. It was inspired by Isaiah 52:2, a text in which God promises to deliver Israel from bondage, and it depicts Mary, the mother of God, as a Jewess. The writer of the icon reflects that, had Mary lived in later years in Nazi Germany, she would have been in a concentration camp with other members of her religion.

Lentz wrote this icon as an act of repentance for Christian indifference, then and now. You may choose to invite a group to compose its own psalm of lamentation out of their pain in this Movement. The verses might begin with phrases such as: "I/We have a complaint, God, about..." or "I/am We/are concerned, God, about..." or "I/We are troubled, God, about..." An appropriate group response could be: "Spirit, be freed and deliver us."

The group could also choose a psalm that has some particular meaning for the group. -- There are no wrong words. Texts can contribute to dialogue and should not be judged on the merits of the

---

[50] Elsa Gidlow, "Chains of Fire." Publication unknown; found in the newsletter of <u>Womanspirit</u>, an Oregon organization no longer in existence.

74

composer or the person suggesting a particular psalm.

The most striking Jewish expression of grief is the rending of garments by the mourner prior to a funeral service. It is an opportunity to vent pent-up anger and anguish. It is a visible, dramatic symbol of the internal tearing that the mourner feels in his/her loss of relationship with the deceased. What is to prevent such symbolic action in spiritual discernment? This action could be done individually or as a group, and it could well be continued throughout the process. Pieces of cloth might gradually form a mosaic that comes to symbolize part of the commonly held story, or corporate memory, of the group.

The same symbolic action could be done by breaking a clay pot or a glass (not someone's prized antique!). Or, individuals could be invited to write what they want to shed on pieces of paper (perhaps rice paper), roll the papers into a cone, set them afire and let the ashes rise like incense into the air. The ashes that remain could be kept in a container as a reminder throughout the remainder of the spiritual discernment process.

The group could also return a clay vessel that they have made into a smooth piece of clay, symbolizing a letting go of their attachments. Or, the group could make the vessel larger, symbolizing openness to the actions of God's Spirit without the impediments they formerly held as important.

There is a familiar and powerful Shaker hymn that could be sung during this Movement: "How Can I Keep from Singing?"

"MY LIFE FLOWS ON IN ENDLESS SONG
ABOVE EARTH'S LAMENTATION.
I HEAR THE REAL THOUGH FAR-OFF HYMN
THAT HAILS A NEW CREATION.

THROUGH ALL THE TUMULT AND THE STRIFE,
I HEAR THAT MUSIC RINGING;
IT SOUNDS AND ECHOES IN MY SOUL;
HOW CAN I KEEP FROM SINGING?

WHAT THOUGH THE TEMPEST 'ROUND ME ROAR,
I HEAR THE TRUTH, IT LIVETH.
WHAT THOUGH THE DARKNESS 'ROUND ME

CLOSE,
SONGS IN THE NIGHT IT GIVETH.

WHEN TYRANTS TREMBLE, SICK WITH FEAR,
AND HEAR THEIR DEATH KNELLS RINGING;
WHEN FRIENDS REJOICE BOTH FAR AND NEAR,
HOW CAN I KEEP FROM SINGING?

THE PEACE OF CHRIST MAKES FRESH MY HEART,
A FOUNTAIN EVER SPRINGING.
ALL THINGS ARE MINE SINCE I AM HIS;
HOW CAN I KEEP FROM SINGING?

REFRAIN:

NO STORM CAN SHAKE MY INMOST CALM,
WHILE TO THAT ROCK I'M CLINGING.
SINCE LOVE IS LORD OF HEAVEN AND EARTH,
HOW CAN I KEEP FROM SINGING?[51]

---

[51] Robert Lowry, How Can I Keep from Singing? Gather Comprehensive,
(Chicago, IL: GIA Publications, Inc., 1989).

> ***ROOTING*** - Naming biblical images or texts and historic events. Given the particular matter for spiritual discernment, what are some biblical images or stories that come to mind? What other stories come to mind from the tradition of your denomination, or your local congregation? *Rooting* in tradition is an experience of remembering things, events and people. It is an opportunity for recalling sacred memories and their meanings.

As ritual and the arts continue to inform a process of spiritual discernment, we become aware that traditions are both stable and fluid. In new settings, faithfulness to tradition often demands reinterpretation or critical analysis of the situation so that our present day actions won't be counter to the Gospel. Developing a friendship with tradition is looking for the best wisdom in a given time or place in our heritage. *Rooting* in tradition is relying on God's Spirit to guide the flow of the process toward deeper insights.

I ministered as a teacher and vice principal in the Mission District of San Francisco in the late 1960's until mid 1970's. It was not long after I first arrived at St. Paul's Parish that I heard the story of the building of the church, and in particular the construction of the two steeples of the church. The steeples are artistically magnificent. They still can be seen in all their splendor rising above the district from Twin Peaks, a tourist spot for viewing the entire city. The steeples have been, however, wrought with tragedy. One's eyes eventually pass down one steeple to the circular gravesite of a worker who fell to his death while helping to construct this visible sign of the church.

The art that this particular person helped to create is in those two magnificent steeples, but it is also in his character and that of the immigrant generations that are part, to this present day, of this faith community. It is this, in its fullness, which those of us who are part of the story attempt to pass on to succeeding generations.

Using elements or symbols from the stories shared, a discernmentarian asks leading questions such as "What are our indwelling spires?" or "What stones in the building of our community are irreplaceable?" Questions such as these will lead the discerners into theological reflection upon their story.

Stories from our congregations or faith traditions introduce us to God's steadfast presence among us. They lead us to consider some possibilities for the future. They coax us to look beyond our limits, and they never fail to hint of a surprise or two.

Dr. Charles M. Olsen in his book, *Transforming Church Boards into Communities of Spiritual Leaders* suggests a very simple and fun way to "Group Tell" a story. Someone begins the story, then others use the connecting words "and then" or "but before that."[52] This method surfaces the "thick" story or history: facts, feelings, pieces of the story unknown to some participants. This theory reflects Mary Benet McKinney's premise in her book entitled *Sharing Wisdom*: everyone has a piece of the wisdom. No one person has all the wisdom.

Clarissa T. Sligh's 1993 composition, *Who We Was*, caran d'Ache crayon on cyanotype and engraved plastic, 90"x240" would be a provocative visual to use during this Movement. It depicts clearly, and in shadows, men, women and children of African descent against a dark eight panel backdrop. The following words are repeated on approximately eighteen horizontal lines behind the figures: "BUT WE KNEW WE WASN'T WHO YOU ALL SAID WE WAS. WE DIDN'T KNOW WHO WE WAS."[53] This is a powerful statement of coming to terms with one's roots. Discerners might be encouraged to share their stories of coming to terms with where they've come from.

Teresa of Avila, the great Christian mystic, writes in her masterpiece *The Interior Castle*: "Not a little misery and confusion arise from the fact that through our own guilt we do not understand ourselves and do not know who we are. Would it not seem a terrible ignorance if one had no answer to give to the question, who one was, who his parents were, and from what country he came? If this were a sign of bestial incomprehension, an incomparably worse stupidity would prevail in us, if we did not take care to learn what we are, but contented ourselves with these bodies, and consequently knew only superficially, from heresay, because faith teaches us, that we had a soul. But what treasures this soul may harbor within it, who dwells in it, and what great value it has, these are things we seldom consider, and hence people are so little concerned

---

[52] Charles M. Olsen. Transforming Church Boards into Communities of Spiritual Leaders. Washington, DC: The Alban Institute, 1995, p 64.
[53] Julio Hiller & Nancy G. Heller, eds. North American Women Artists of the 20th Century, a Biographical Dictionary. New York & London: Garland Publishing, Inc., 1995, p 514.

with preserving their beauty with all care."[54]

Just over a year ago facilitated a process with sixteen members of the Board of Directors of my religious congregation. The issue was as extensive piece of land and a large building which was a formation house for some of our youngest members. This property had been on the market for a number of years, its potential sale had reached stalemate after stalemate, and we needed to look at new options for its sale.

The process I developed integrated the "practices" in "worshipful-work" and some specific Movements in spiritual discernment. Since we couldn't tell the story of this property over the last decade in less than many hours, I decided to invite the story to be told in this way: *"Reflect for a moment on _____. Think of your associations with this piece of land, with persons who shared time there with you, with particular meetings or events held there, with the buildings on the premesis. -- I invite you to reverently share just words or phrases that come to you."*

This storytelling took approximately forty-five minutes. It was profound. Names of significant people and events were shared, as were feelings of gratitude and of loss. Tears were shed, and feelings of peace rose from the pain. After a quiet break, we were able to name some themes that ran through "our story" and also identify some stories from Scripture that reflect similar persons and events. We chose one story to weave with our story in biblical, and later, theological reflection.

Our stories throughout history produce theology, a growing understanding of God, and God's life in our midst. Telling our stories, even those ripe with the advantage of many years of hindsight, reveals the deeper and richer motifs of a community, and they produce rituals. These rituals signify the intrinsic parts, the signs, actions and gestures of our stories.

A discernmentarian may invite a group to construct a banner or a mobile or a windsock illustrating the biblical images or texts and/or historic events that have been shared--and now owned corporately--by the group. Can a particular theme or a charism for the group be named and then symbolized on the banner, mobile or windsock, or painted on a gourd?

Should your gathering take place during the season of Advent, a

---

[54] Teresa of Avila, The Interior Castle. Trans. Kieran Kavanaugh & Otilio Rodriguez. New York, NY: 1979, p 36.

Jesse Tree made from a tree branch and planted in a pot, or made with a live, spindly plant, can be decorated with symbols for those persons who "lived before us and prepared the way." The symbols or drawings of biblical ancestors and/or local community members can be made of any type of material and hung on the branches with yarn or string. Storytelling should take place while the symbols are being constructed and hung on the tree.

Joining a particular Scripture passage with its compliment in song is a way of reinforcing the message of the passage. Let me suggest some examples. First Corinthians, Chapter 12, speaks of God's people having many spiritual gifts, but having gifts that differ: "There are varieties of gifts but the same Spirit...To each is given the manifestation of the Spirit for the common good" (verses 4,7). Why not add to the impact of that message by singing "There Is One Lord", or "We Are Many Parts", or "In Christ There Is No East Or West?"

Some of the texts we sing during Sunday worship are acclamations and psalms. They are usually simple, easily remembered responses with which we are at home. Why not sing them as a blessing for persons after they have told their story or shared something significant with the group? An *Amen*, or an *Alleluia*, a *Thanks be to God* or a *Lord, Have Mercy* that is sung by heart centers the group in its experience of God present in the moment.

Inviting participants to periodically choose a hymn from their church hymnal that expresses in song what the group is experiencing is another way to involve each member. The group may choose to sing a refrain, selected verses, or the entire hymn. "One Bread, One Body" by John Foley, reminds us that we are one though different in many ways. "The Church Is One Foundation" carries similar meaning with the added historical dimension.

I suggest staying away from selecting music, art or poetry that is triumphal or pietistic. Spiritual discernment deals with real life issues and should not be subjected to a Hollywood veneer or escapism of any kind. The arts should only serve the process of spiritual discernment, helping to form true integration of mind, body and spirit.

Being a native of Seattle, I've grown up with an appreciation for--and fascination with--totem poles. A totem pole, read from the top down, is like a pictorial family genealogy or directory. Each figure on the pole represents a member of the family, similar to what you find on a family crest. The portrayed animal figures are based on the

80

characteristics of the animal most admired by the person being represented.

It has been the tradition for each tribe to have a professional carver, someone who inherits the tribe's legends. Carvers have always been important members of a tribe and are well paid for their work. Families that want their own totem pole hire the tribal carver and contribute family stories to the artisan's process. Once the totem pole is completed, the family displays it outside their home.

It is not beyond my imagination to conceive of persons or groups in spiritual discernment creating their own "totem" story. As the earliest writings of native Americans were signs and symbols, our present day liturgical life can also provide abundant signs. Let the following Native American symbols prime the pump for your own use of symbols:

- *Sun rays* image constancy; the *lasso*, captivity.
  "In this spiritual discernment process, what do we need to shed?"
- The *butterfly* symbolizes life, and *running water*, constant life. *Morning stars* symbolize guidance.
  "In our process and as we connect with our stories, how are we being confronted, nudged, or confirmed?"
- A *tepee* stands for a temporary home, a *hogan* a permanent home. *Raindrops* symbolize plentiful crops and *rain clouds*, good prospects.
  "Is our discernment matter resting in the heart?" *"Or, does it have the feeling of a temporary home?"*

Other symbols, can also be used. A *bear track* stands for a good omen. *Crossed arrows* are symbols of friendship. What nationalities encompass the participants in the group, and what are their meaningful symbols?

The Heyse Center of the National Museum of the American Indian in New York City, has an exhibit entitled *Agyuliyaraput (Our Way of Making Prayer): The Living Tradition of Yup'ik Masks*. The masks were made by Yup'ik Eskimos. Is there a mask that you or a participant could share with the group? Could you request a loan from a local museum or library? The Metropolitan Museum in New York City publishes a unique book entitled *MASKS*. The book contains five realistic, three-dimensional masks, illustrations of more than forty works of art plus maps, photographs and commentary by Museum curators.

Masks can serve to display pride in heritage. What story can be told of a mask you've chosen for its quality of art? The group in discernment could choose to design and decorate one large mask. Since symbols on the mask need to reflect heritage, some quality conversation should take place before and while the mask is being created. Later, the mask could be displayed on a wall or in another artistic arrangement, one that remains throughout the process of discernment as a visual reminder of keeping grounded and rooted in tradition.

John Giuliani, who lives in a small monastic community in West Redding, Connecticut hadn't picked up a paintbrush in thirty-six years when he took a class by a Russian Orthodox icon painter in 1989. After a few months of study, Giuliani had what he describes as a "eureka" moment. "I suddenly began to wonder what I was doing using traditional Byzantine aesthetics and forms, living as I do in North America in the late Twentieth Century. Then the idea came to me of using the images of the continent's original peoples in icons, as a way of celebrating the spiritual gifts they have given to the world. ... As his work has become better known, Giuiani admits to at first feeling a bit apprehensive about the Indian response, worrying that some might dismiss the icons as simply another example of American colonization of native culture. Instead, I've been overjoyed [to see] how much it means to them to see their faces and traditions portrayed as holy."[55]

Today, Giuliani's icons, which synthesize traditional iconography with images of native Americans, draws praise from Native Americans and art critics alike. Giuliani is quoted as saying: "An icon is an invitation. It can be a true mediational presence, a means to move into the mystery of the sacred. I would like my icons to be seen as Alice's looking glass, mirrors that allow both reflection and entrance into the transcendent--the sacred that exists in us all." [56]

Note cards and posters of Giuliani's work are available from Bridge Building Images, Box 1048, Burlington, VT 05402; 1-800-325-6263. The sale of his artwork helps support his community and an ecumenical soup kitchen, of which he is the founder and director.

Given the national roots of the persons in discernment, what artwork will resonate well with the group?

---

[55] Lori Erickson, "A Window To The Sacred," Sojourners Magazine, March/April, 1997, pp. 48, 51.

[56] Ibid. p 51.

Robert Lentz, whom I mentioned earlier in conjunction with the use of icons in spiritual discernment, has written many contemporary icons which have universal appeal but which have special meaning for particular nationalities. His *Mohandas Gandhi, Oscar Romero,* and *Mother Jones*, all depict people who worked most of their lives for the poor and oppressed, and in some cases, ended up shedding their blood for the cause of justice and peace. Lentz has also created the *Celtic Trinity*, which depicts three women of three different races with a serpent and a raven, symbols of the cycles of life and death. There is plenty of food for thought in each of these icons.

A stroll through an art gallery or a sculpture garden is another possible source of artistic reflection during this *Rooting* in tradition Movement. The Sheldon Memorial Art Gallery and Sculpture Garden located at the University of Nebraska in Lincoln, has among its sculptures *Pieta*, by Bruno Lucchesi (1970) and *Serenity*, by Saul Baigesnar (1932-29). The Storm Key Art Center, located on a four hundred acre park on the Hudson River, has a sculpture park with over one hundred twenty masterworks by sculptors including David Smith, Isamu Noguchi, Alexander Calder, and Louise Nevelson.

There is a wonderful hymn entitled "Seeds of Change" by Carolyn McDade which jumps right into the heart of the *Rooting* Movement: "This is a time we honor and name those who gathered before us...This is a time we hear God's word in the voices never heard who shatter all myths of pretention....Cycles move; people can change, turning fresh in the morning...Blossoms of joy amidst the pain...Love that died is born again and sacred all lands and all peoples. ... A time to plow, a time to sow, a time to tend, a time to let grow, gather, lay fallow, then turn the earth again."[57]

How better to recall sacred people, memories and their meanings than by *Rooting* them in sung tradition.

---

[57] Carolyn McDade. Sister, Carry On. Wellfleet, MA: Carolyn McDade and Friends, 1992.

Chapter Four

Weaving Ritual & The Arts Throughout The Movements Of Listening -- Exploring -- Improving

These three Movements, *Listening*, *Exploring* and *Improving* illustrate *Cultivating the Plants* in spiritual discernment. During these Movements it is important to incorporate intentional times of silent and spoken prayer, lest the individual or group feel a sense of urgency to move forward too quickly. It is also important to pray to God in gratitude for being in a place of unknowing, a place challenging us to trust in God's grace and be open to God's favors.

Time is the gift given in spiritual discernment. This gift is not to be stifled or rushed. We need the awareness time gives us -- of being in the sacred hollow of God's hands.

CULTIVATING THE PLANTS

"A farmer patiently cultivates the plants. The nutrients in the soil, the light and air from the sky and the moisture from the rains enable the young plant to appropriate these resources, stretch, expand, and come to maturity. ...Discernment is cultivated through listening, appropriating all the information and wisdom that is available from God and each other. Explore every possible option to see if God is in it. Work to improve each option."[58]

---

[58] Charles M. Olsen and Danny E. Morris. <u>Discerning God's Will Together: A Spiritual Practice for the Church</u>. Washington, D.C.: The Alban Institute; Nashville, TN: The Upper Room, 1997, pp. 69,70.

> *LISTENING* – "What voices do we need to hear?" The
> *Listening* Movement includes a gathering of information as well
> as an awareness of the inner promptings in oneself and others
> that need to be heard. Be eager to learn from *Listening* because
> God will be encountered in a variety of voices.

Spiritual discernment entails a deep *Listening to* God, to the
voices of persons who are in the middle of the matter being discerned, as
well as to the cries of the people who will be affected by the impact of
the outcome or decision. It is through this *Listening* Movement that we
come to know the patterns inherent in ways we unite and connect, not
unlike the broccoli buds Margaret Wheatley so aptly describes in
Leadership and the New Science. Resorting to the use of a multiplicity
of listening opportunities should provide a more diverse and wiser pool
of information for decision making via discernment. This Movement has
a lot to do with openness to the unknown and to change.

In spiritual discernment, effective listeners possess an
unquenchable "What's around the corner?" interest. Effective listeners
ask more questions than most people, and they listen for the "Why?"
behind the "What?" Discernmentarians and discerners show curiosity by
being quicker with queries than proclamations. They intentionally avoid
judgmental tones since they know they will learn more with invitation
and acceptance than with evaluation and accusation. Their deep listening
begins with internal inquiry and thoughtful, prayerful reflection.

You may be familiar with walking a labryinth. A labryinth can
be walked in individual solitude or as part of a group. It can be walked
during this *Listening* Movement and periodically throughout a process of
spiritual discernment. One approach to this prayerful walk is the
following: As you walk toward the center, let go of the details and
concerns of your life. Quiet your mind and open your heart. (*Release.*)
The center is a place of quiet or meditation. It is here that you may find
insight. (*Illumination.*) Follow the path out. You may feel grounded and
energized at this time. Try to integrate the insights gained in the center.
(*Union*).

"In a seventeenth-century Chinese treatise on painting, called
The Mustard Seed Garden Manual, the artist is advised to compose his
picture so that if, say, he is painting a man looking at a mountain, the
man will appear to be bent in an attitude of homage and the mountain

85

will itself appear to be slightly bent in an attitude of acknowledgement. Or if a lutist is playing her instrument under the moon, the painter is advised to make it appear that the lutist is listening to the moon and the moon is listening to her. The spiritual presupposition of this counsel is that humans stand in a relation of reciprocity with the world and that like them, all of the world is instinct with spirit and presence, the numinous and the sacred. As such, it must be treated with reverence and respect."[59]

Since *Listening* in spiritual discernment entails encountering a variety of voices, it might be well to continue the dialogue about the particular stage of group development the participants are in before entering completely into this Movement (ref. p 16). *Listening*, especially to differing viewpoints, or to people with whom there may be a history of disagreement, will call for a greater amount of openness and trust than in the past. Reflection on the stages of group development could preface an invitation to write a personal behavioral statement, e.g., "I will...', or "I won't...", or "I will try...". These statements, when listened to and shared with the whole group, will help to build the group's trust level.

The skills specific to *Listening* include *Attending, Following* and *Responding*, and basic to each of these components is the ability to engage in reflection. I will comment specifically on each of these components and on the capacity for reflection.

Attending means paying close attention and being sensitive to cues within oneself, other persons, and within the environment that speak to the situation. Attend, translated into Greek, is diakonos, the term for ministry. So, being *attending* is being engaged in ministry, or in service. The early Christians were an attending community; they recognized the plight of the poor and the sick in their midst and made it their goal to respond appropriately.

To be *attending* is to offer hospitality. There is an icon made in Wisconsin at an Orthodox Skete entitled *The Hospitality of Abraham*, (available from Religious Resources International 3695 S. Shady Lane, New Berlin, WI 53146), which shows Abraham and Sarah entertaining their three mysterious visitors. This icon is a good centering focus for a discernmentarian, for to offer hospitality to the "travelers" in discernment is to entertain God's ongoing life in their midst.

Following may be described as companionship, a walking

---

[59] Maria Harris. Proclaim Jubilee, A Spirituality for the Twenty-First Century. Louisville, KY: Westminster John Knox Press, 1996, p 24.

alongside and learning from one's environment. It does not mean being in the way or imposing an opinion. It is shown in words and body language. It is letting others know that we'd really like to hear what they have to say because they are important and their story is worth telling.

Responding involves an appropriate and understanding response. Jesus' response to the Samaritan woman in John's Gospel (4:7-30) is a perfect example of an appropriate, understanding and very compassionate response. Jesus revealed details about the woman that she had not previously shared with him. His response was, in fact, so reflective that it happened regardless of the fact that it stood in direct opposition to the culture of the times. The Samaritan woman came away from that encounter knowing she had been totally understood. The disciples, on the other hand, remained puzzled because they could only see externally what happened.

Companionship happens when a person is able to move beyond ruminating on a situation (dwelling on something, or going over and over in one's mind the concrete details of what happened) to reflection on the situation. The capacity for reflection means being able to leave the obvious facts or details (why it happened and how it happened), and search for the significance, the deeper meaning of the event.

Remember how important unhurried time is to this and all the Movements in spiritual discernment? As the group you are working with engages in the Movements of *Listening*, *Exploring* and *Improving*, invite the writing poetry or journal writing about the "gift of time" to engage in the process. The purpose of this exercise is for persons to actively engage in their own significant journey in discernment, as well as to reflect on the process itself. Discerners might discover that this exercise brings significant insights, and some persons may choose to share their writings with the group.

For background music, consider using Vivaldi's *The Four Seasons*, choosing the music that corresponds to the season of the year, i.e., "Autumn", No. 3 in F. Vivaldi's concertos are generally familiar, yet they seem to become something new each time they are heard. They are musical paintings that cause us to hear and imagine new things.

I'm surmising that the author of the following poem, a former colleague, wasn't thinking about the Movements in spiritual discernment when he was writing his poetic work. He was by nature a reflective person and always openly grateful for the gift of life, so I'll take this opportunity to share one of his gifts with you. It is entitled "Time":

"Every time
I see a clock
I breathe a prayer
On the fleeting hands.

I don't ask for time
To finish my work,
To live on earth,
To enjoy its blessings.

I don't ask for time
To rush ahead
To some uncertain date,
For God is served in an endless now.

I don't ask for time
To drag along,
Fearful of the morrow's call:
To tarry here is to bypass heaven.

I ask only for Wisdom
To use each hour,
Each day, each now,
As best I can.

Each moment is dear;
I'll do in it what I can
It will never return.
Nor, my yesterdays will you. "[60]

The group might also spend some time doing biblical and theological reflection on some of the sayings of Jesus. Irony was one of Jesus' favorite teaching tools, i.e., "Truly I tell you, it will be hard for a rich person to enter the kingdom of heaven. Again I tell you, it is easier

---

[60] R. Dave Bielefeld. <u>Montana Priest</u>. Unpublished collection, 1988, p 8.

for a camel to go through the eye of a needle than for someone who is rich to enter the kingdom of God." (Mt 19:23-24) Delve into the deeper meaning of this or other passages with a focused conversation: "What strikes you about this passage?" "What is it saying that concerns you?" "What new insight about this passage excites you?" Of course, the inclusion of humor is always welcome.

Or, choose a biblical poem to ponder as a group. The 150 songs to which we commonly give the name of "psalms", and the "canticles", other poems similar in structure, content or style scattered throughout the Jewish and Christian Scriptures, serve to light the path of discernment. They are our common cry of memory and hope, of praise and pain, of confidence and fear. We are brought together by the human realities they articulate; we can find one another's truth in their lines. Read a psalm or canticle for the overall effect; note the form and the structure; analyze and appreciate individual words and figures of speech, then deduce a theme or a theological point. Be sensitive to the emotions in the poem because poetry is contextualized and nuanced by our human emotions and experiences. Recovery of the spiritual power of any part of this heritage of ancient religious poetry is intimately tied to unlocking our spiritual energy.

You might invite members of the discernment group to imagine themselves as an instrument perfectly attuned to God's Spirit. Ask them to illustrate what this would look like in a pencil sketch. Then, after some silence, invite them to share what glimpses of God's grace they were just given.

Or, individuals may be invited to journal about their experience in one of a variety of ways, i.e.: a dialogue with God, or with a wisdom figure in the community; with an imaginary person in the next generation; with someone who has been disenfranchised. A follow-up question for reflection followed by dialogue could be simply: "What did you hear?"

A few years ago, I participated in a reflection on the charism of the foundress of my religious congregation, Mary Frances Clarke. Years of initial and continuing formation contributed to this experience, so it was not, for any of the participants, an introduction to the spirituality of our congregation . It was, however, a unique experience. The facilitator constructed a creative environment, surrounding us with elements and articles of Mary Frances' life: a quill pen she used, a shawl she had worn in the mid to late 1800's to ward off the cold, some of her early handwritten letters and prayers, and a copy of her rule book.

After some leading reflection questions, silent prayer and a period of inner dialogue/journaling with Mary Frances, we were asked to share what we heard her saying to us individually and to our congregation. The *Listening* was profound. It assisted our personal growth and deepened our identity as members of the same community. We were able to more deeply understand how our individual giftedness intersects creatively and harmoniously with the "spirit of the congregation." To use Margaret Wheatley's methaphor, we experienced our "fields", the invisible structures which gives our group a certain recognizable identity. These "fields" have outlasted Mary Frances and the group who generated it in 1833. In a process of spiritual discernment, we try to discover if our personal and corporate fields are mutually compatible and enriching, or not.

I once participated in a group process during which, over several days, each person created her own "Dream Catcher." Legendary dream catchers are said to entangle bad dreams in their webs and let good dreams travel through the center hole. During this *Listening* Movement, you may wish to provide each participant with a small frame and an assortment of leather pieces, feathers and beads. Following the construction of the webbed frames, invite the addition of other elements which signify inner promptings (or voices heard) at any time throughout this Movement. Be sure to share their significance with the whole group.

Anselm Keifer painted *Interior* in 1981. It is a painting of an oblong room that appears to be an atrium. Tree branches are visible through the glass portion of the ceiling. The walls are of dark wood, and there is a person on a stand against one wall who is obviously busy about painting or cleaning the wood. The spaciousness of the room and the position of the man reminds me of discerners listening to all voices in all corners, and on both sides of the walls.

To whom should individuals and the group be *Listening*? "What wisdom figures need to be heard?" "Are there wisdom figures both at the center of our experience and on the edge?" "What writings should we read?" "What photographs should we view that tell some of the story?" "What artifacts should we observe?"

"Change Our Hearts", by Rory Cooney, or "Standin' in the Need of Prayer", the African-American spiritual, are examples of sung prayer that can be catalysts for awakening a deep resonance to listen with God's longing for us. Sing these songs or others like them with or without accompaniment; harmonize if you'd like; sing with all your hearts, then spend time in silence. A calming refrain that could be intersperced as sung prayer is " Spirit of the living God, fall afresh on me. Spirit of the living God, fall afresh on me."[61] The verses could also be sung, and the personal pronouns could be alternated or sing the final verse using "us."

EXPLORING - "What are some options within the Guiding Principle?" There will be some obvious options. What others are possible? Allow for new insights and surprises. Allow for some give-and-take between this Movement and the others, especially *Rooting, Shedding* and *Listening.* Don't let some usual ways of decision making interfere with efforts to correlate explorations of the matter at hand with the wisdom of our Christian tradition. Surrender to the mystery of the future.

One of the hoped for outcomes of spiritual discernment is growth, not just superficial change. Persons who take spiritual discernment seriously, who practice it as a natural way of being, won't ever become like inanimate, porous sponges with extraneous material that never becomes a real part of them. They will not act like crustaceans (clams or oysters) living within shells that admits no more growth. If oysters and clams opened their solid and restricting coverings, they could become prey to anything in the ocean. Paradoxically they don't grow, but their lives are protected!

In spiritual discernment we need to seek out the various paths or options available to us—even those more uncertain paths--and not avoid looking at them. We will be misguided if we use our imaginations as a means to slide into denial. This *Exploring* Movement is not meant to blind us to what might be honest but painful facts. It is meant to illumine the larger issues, to encourage rather than curb imaginative leaps. To see with the eyes of our imaginations we need a kind of double vision, a vision that allows us to examine concepts such as tradition and change, security and risk. We peer as through binoculars, telescopes,

---

[61] Daniel Iverson, Spirit of the Living God, The Presbyterian Hymnal, (Louisville, KY: Westminster/John Knox Press, 1990).

microscopes and colored lenses for ways to deepen our appreciation of the grace and force of ideas, and develop the art of throwing them into fresh combinations.

Oliver Wendell Holmes, Jr.'s well known saying: "I find the great thing in this world is not so much where we stand, as in what direction we are moving"[62] gives us some impetus for this movement. In spiritual discernment, God's Spirit is luring and calling us to play with possibilities, to explore and discover new options. As long as we are alive on earth we are on our way, choosing our options for a road trip that is yet unfinished because we have unlimited potential for personal growth. Unfinished because there are mysteries always awaiting us as we live into God. In spiritual discernment we need to be open to possibilities and mysteries, to welcome the unexpected. This is what will make the journey an adventure!

What are some questions a discernmentarian might pose during this *Exploring* Movement? Let me name but a few: "How do we understand the paradox of stability and freedom with regard to...?" "Does our emphasis seem to be on survival or on emergence?" "Do we believe in caution more than in surprise?" "Is our information *in*-formation?" "Is our dialogue frozen, or incapable of being transformed by developing insights?" "How are we engaging each other in order to evoke creativity?" "What other people are repositories of wisdom for us?" "Which option will cause us to thrive rather than just survive?"

Since persons in discernment strive to value their relationships with each other, with God and within the system (congregation, denomination, etc.) of which they are an integral part, it is well to periodically focus on these relationships, noting how they can change us and evoke more from us. When we do this, our spirituality becomes more visible, even to ourselves.

American artists began experimenting with a new printmaking medium during the latter part of the Nineteenth Century. American painter Charles Alvah Walker gave the process the name *monotype*. The technique entails drawing or painting an image on a surface such as a metal plate, then transferring the image through pressure to a sheet of paper (similar to the making of a *rubbing* with chalk or crayon on onionskin paper). The result is a mirror-image impression. Currently, The National Museum of American Art features a show entitled

---

[62] Oliver Wendell Holmes. The Aristocrat of the Breakfast Table. 1891, p 93.

"Singular Impressions: The Monotype in America", in which an untitled landscape c. 1885 by artist Joseph Jefferson is displayed. This landscape is also featured in "Smithsonian Highlights" on page 30 of the May, 1997 Smithsonian magazine. The print shows a woman with a basket in her arms walking into a forest. A discernmentarian may ask the group the following questions in the form of a guided meditation:

"Place yourself in the picture as that person carrying that basket. * Do you choose to go down that obvious path, or clearing? * What are you looking for on the path you choose? * What are you finding? * Are there any surprises?"

Annie Dillard, a profound and fresh writer who exhibits a mature astonishment at the presence of God in all of life, writes in *Pilgrim at Tinker Creek* a statement that is pertinent to the *Exploring* Movement: "Our life is a faint tracing on the surface of mystery, like the idle, curved tunnels of leaf miners on the face of a leaf. We must take a wider view, look at the whole landscape, really see it, and describe what's going on here. Then we can at least wail the right question into the swaddling band of darkness, or, if it comes to that, choir the proper praise."[63]

What paths are available on the face of the group's leaf? Name them. Let your creative juices flow. Don't just be practical and methodical. "What option/s make me/us feel enlivened? Make me/us feel stifled?"

Consider the sunrise. It cannot be hurried. Early risers suspect the sun is just below the horizon because the glow seems so faint. More minutes pass, and the border grows red and more colorful in the east. As time goes by, the band of colorful light creeps upward from the line where our earth met the sky, intensifying more in color and bending the horizon in front of the waters.

Remember that our horizon is the only one we see! Challenge the group in spiritual discernment to bend their horizons: look to what is just beneath the surface, what dim light, images, possibilities are surfacing? Stretch not only minds, but also bodies, as you invite the group to take a quick walk and come back refreshed to look at new possibilities.

One of my favorite outdoor places is in Federal Way,

---

[63] Annie Dillard. Pilgrim at Tinker Creek. New York: Harper & Row Publishers, 1974, p 9.

Washington. It is the home of The Pacific Rim Bonsai Collection, a living museum of ninety of the nation's most elite dwarf trees magnificently displayed in sun-dappled woods on Weyerhaeuser's corporate campus. The trees have roots in China, Taiwan, Korea, Japan, Canada and the United States. Among them there is a famous Surinam cherry entitled *Holding Up the Sky*, a graceful tree with delicate leaves whose trunk soaring skyward represents the ascending human spirit. There is also a 180-year-old trident maple that weathered bankruptcy and repossession in the 1929 stock market crash and then survived years of neglect when its Japanese-American owner was relocated to an internment camp during World War II. There is a purple-leaf flowering plum, a Japanese gray bark elm, a weeping tamarisk in a special pot that bears the crest of the Japanese emperor, an eastern larch collected from Nova Scotia's Dead Crow Lake. All of the trees are artistic sculptures. They each have dramatic personalities. They are old, some even ancient. Some are twisted by wind, bent with time, burdened by snow. Dead wood suggests the trees have survived adversity and made it; soft shoots add new beauty to their history. They elicit in the viewer an entire landscape; they have the power to send the viewer on an imaginary journey.

Is there such a natural sculpture path in your area through which the discernment group can take a journey? In my experience of walking through The Pacific Rim Bonsai Collection I've found that it elicits emotions, recaptures scenes or moments in my life, and unpredictably evokes or releases tensions. It also soothes my soul and lifts my spirits.

I have recently become more familiar with the paintings of George de La Tour, who often chose beggars or impoverished musicians as subjects for his art. La Tour, who was noted for his antisocial behaviors, lived during the time of the Counter-Reformation, when the Catholic Church was making every effort to counter the challenge of Protestantism. New churches and new religious orders were taking hold. "One of the striking aspects of his religious art was that often the men and women who peopled his canvases might have been encountered in the village square or the Friday fish market. They were neighbors transformed, indeed exalted, by belief and repentance."[64] They were folks just like us.

---

[64] Helen Dudar, "From Darkness into Light: Rediscovering George de La Tour," Smithsonian Magazine, December, 1996, p 80.

94

Although lacking conventional religious trappings, La Tour's austere *Newborn Child* from the mid-1640's, is a painting capable of deeply moving its viewers. Illuminated by a single candle, the figure takes on a monumental quality. One woman, cast in the shadows except for her face and chest, has her hand raised in a gesture of blessing the swaddled child. The woman holding the child, sitting in awe of its being, is covered in subtle light and gentle shadows.

La Tour chose as one of his most popular subjects, Mary Magdalene, an extraordinary figure in early Christianity and in all likelihood a disciple parallel to Peter. La Tour's 1635 painting, *The Magdalene at the Mirror*, captures her shadowed body confronting her image in a mirror. She is in an obviously pensive mood, one hand placed on a dark image of a skull. She appears to be questioning what is of earthly and/or heavenly value. All Christians, male and female, may find images such as these helpful to ponder as they search and sort within themselves for deeper meanings in a process of spiritual discernment. Viewing La Tour's art, you may wish to ask questions such as these: "What can I learn from seeing myself as Mary Magdalene? Or the woman in the shadow? Or the woman blessing the child?"

The icon *Saint Mary Magdalene* by Robert Lentz (1990) was commissioned for Grace Cathedral in San Francisco to commemorate the election of Barbara Harris, the first woman bishop in the Anglican communion. The icon is striking, not only for the manner in which Mary Magdalene is portrayed, but for the vivid and rich colors used in its writing. Lentz has this commentary about the icon: "According to the ancient tradition of the East, Mary Magdalene was a wealthy woman from whom Christ expelled seven "demons." During the three years of Jesus' ministry she helped support him and his other disciples with her money. When almost everyone else fled, she stayed with him at the cross. On Easter morning she was the first to bear witness to his resurrection. She is called "Equal to the Apostles." The Eastern tradition tells us that after the Ascension she journeyed to Rome where she was admitted to the court of Tiberias Caesar because of her high social standing. After describing how poorly Pilate had administered justice at Jesus' trial, she told Caesar that Jesus had risen from the dead. To help explain his resurrection she picked up an egg from the dinner table. Caesar responded that a human being could no more rise from the dead than the egg in her hand turn red. The egg turned red immediately, which is why red eggs have been exchanged at Easter for centuries in the

Byzantine East. ... As women reclaim their ancient rights in the church, Mary Magdalene challenges all Christians to re-examine their cultural prejudices about gender and leadership."[65]

During the *Exploring* Movement, while meditating on one of the above mentioned paintings, the discernmentarian might ask: "What is to become of choosing this particular path, or giving birth to this idea?" "How might it mature?" "What light and darkness lies ahead?" "Who will support and nourish this idea?" "What is our prayer as we dream about this future?"

Prayers of intercession could be offered beginning with "I/We imagine that...". After a moment of quiet, a response might be "God, graciously hear our prayer."

There is a provocative picture available, matted or framed, from the Sojourners Resource Center (2401 15th Street NW, Washington, DC 20009; 800-714-7474) that could well be used by a group discerning an issue involving social justice. It shows a gray figure sitting on a park bench. In black calligraphy on a white background is printed Matthew 25:40: "Inasmuch a you have done it unto one of the least of these my brethren, you have done it unto me." Persons in spiritual discernment may be invited to imagine themselves sitting on that bench. As each avenue is being explored, ask: "What still needs to be seen from this park bench?" "What might we be overlooking?" "Are we considering our emotions or spirits as well as the facts in each path?" "Do any new approaches come to mind?"

During autumn, I enjoy creating dried arrangements of leaves and weeds. As discernmentarian, you might begin an arrangement and invite members of the group to add to it over the course of their time together. Being in touch with nature's transitions allows us to engage ever more deeply in our own inner transitions as we engage in the Movements of spiritual discernment. Invite participants to choose particular leaves or weeds for the ways in which they symbolize particular paths. Arrange them in a vase, on a cloth, or as a map on the wall or carpet.

Are you in a setting where you could take a walk together? If not, invite the discerners to find a twig, leaf, anything whatsoever, near home or work and bring it to the next gathering. Then, before each piece

---

[65] Robert Lentz. Saint Mary Magdalene. Burlington, VT: Bridge Building Images, Inc., 1990.

96

is added to the arrangement, invite comments on the significance of each contribution--why they chose it (in light of its shape, color, composition, etc.). I suspect that the stories they share will be inspired, often profound. The comments will also serve to instruct the group in the integrity of God's creation.

Guided Imagery is a prayer form that may well serve as a way to let God's Spirit creatively work within individuals during this Movement. I have led a group using *The God Tree* (source unknown) in times of discernment. Other helpful examples abound, including some contained in *That I May See: A Prayerful Discovery through Imagination*, by Salvino Briffa. You may wish to write your own guided imagery using a sculpture, or drawing, or a symbol as the focal point with which to center group reflection.

Imagine how a group or an individual might creatively explore the options in this Movement using the following guided imagery around a common stone:

Look at this stone. It is a piece of eternity. Think of how many Centuries of human history this stone has seen and outlived. (Pause, perhaps passing the stone around the group.) *Now close your eyes and picture this same stone. * In your imagination, peel back the layers of this simple stone. * Wonder about all it has seen in its lifetime. * In what way does this stone reflect God? What can it tell you about God? What characteristics of God does it reveal to you? * Imagine yourself as this stone. * If you could roll down one particular path at this point in our discernment, which path would you choose? Which path seems to be of God? * Return now in silence to this room and this holy meeting space. ***

These or similar questions will prompt dialogue within the group: "Tell us about your stone." "What did it teach you about God?" "Which path seemed to be of God and why?"

The use of Guided Imagery followed by simple questions such as those above, or even more simply, "Tell us what you would like to about your meditation", leads persons and the group as a whole to explore more in depth the possible options or paths. Again, there are no wrong statements; there are only insights to be shared.

We may tend to believe that the ordinary and the extraordinary cannot meet. Yet, in fact, we cannot find our religious nature outside of the settings of our human experiences. Letting God's Spirit loose in our prayer during the *Exploring* Movement is like no other opportunity on the horizon.

If those in discernment have constructed a paper or fabric Origami sculpture during a other Movements, it is most appropriate that the sculpture be embellished with decorative beads, other fabric remnants or appropriate materials during this *Exploring* Movement. Likewise, a balloon sculpture or wire mesh sculpture might be properly enhanced during this time. And too, a found art sculpture capable of motion might be further balanced and made more flexible.

Bobby Fisher has written a wonderful hymn based on Micah 6:8 and Psalm 25 called "Servant Song." While singing it we pray for openness to be led in the path of truth. We pray for wisdom. We pray for God to mold our hearts for all that is good. What significant words with which to beseech God's Spirit! Other hymns from your faith tradition will also assist a group in *Exploring* among the various paths or options.

I know of a few churches that have had hymns commissioned and composed specifically for their use. They reflect the church's mission statement, its charism and/or the name of the church. If this is true in your situation, the hymn could be incorporated into various Movements, but certainly the *Exploring* Movement. It will help answer these questions: "How is our Guiding Principle reflected in each of these options?" "Is each option consistent with our charism?"

IMPROVING – or "bettering up": to work together to improve upon every option until each becomes, through mutual consultation and prayer, the very best it can be. This *Improving* Movement calls for comparing, contrasting and developing options.

Something new is unfolding during the duration of a process of spiritual discernment. Research, and subsequent *Exploring* of options, has taken place. It is now in the *Improving* Movement that we attempt to better each option under consideration. This is not foreign territory. It is not unlike our understanding of the marvels that enfold in nature. Alpine ice, which scoured the land for thousand of years, eventually deepened valleys, sculpted their walls and created majestic cliffs and waterfalls, rivers and lakes. When we view these marvels of nature we might well see beyond what ever seemed possible at the very first glance.

In spiritual discernment, we cannot be satisfied with initial options; we need to give time to improve each of these options--time in silence, time in prayer, time in dialogue. We may well need to consult again with those who are to be affected by the discerned outcome, and by those wisdom figures who often have new insights to add to our probings.

A poem that has become a visual image of the *Improving* Movement for me is Annie Dillard's "Life on the Rocks":

> *"Like boys on dolphins*
> *the continents ride their crustal plates.*
> *New lands shoulder up*
> *from the waves and*
> *old lands buckle under.*
> *The very landscapes heave -*
> *   change burgeons into change.*
> *The mountains tremble,*
> *ice rasps back and forth,*
> *up the rock valleys and down,*
> *ramifying possibilities,*
> *riddling the mountains.*

Life and the rocks, like spirit and matter,
are a fringed matrix, lapped and lapping,
clasping and held.
   It is like hand washing hand.
It is like hand washing hand -
the whole tumult hurled.
The planet spins,
rapted inside its intricate mists.
The galaxy is a flung thing,
loose in the night.
Our solar system is
one of many dotted campfires
ringed with tossed rocks.
   What shall we sing?"[66]

"What shall we sing--what shall we say--after we've considered the "many dotted campfires"? "After we've considered "spirit and matter?" "What values are implied in each of our options?" "Are they our ultimate values?"

Following this dialogue, the group's prayer could reside in this familiar tune from the musical *Godspell*, based on the Gospel of Matthew: "Day by day, dear Lord, three things I pray. To see Thee more clearly, love Thee more dearly, follow Thee more nearly, day by day."[67]

It might be helpful during this *Improving* Movement to engage the participants in dialogue with such questions as these: "What image or words/phrases capture the vision that we are after?" "What new attitudes might we need to adopt if we change one or more options, or a particular piece of an option?"

Fritz Eichenberg (1901-1990), a refugee from Nazi Germany and a convert to Quakerism, was one of the world's master wood engravers. He illustrated many Russian literary classics including works by Dostoevsky and Tolstoy, and he contributed an extensive body of work

---

[66] Anne Dillard. Teaching A Stone To Talk. New York: Harper & Row Publishers, 1982, p 130.
[67] John Michael Tbelak. Godspell. Stephen Schwartz, music.

to *The Catholic Worker*, a pacifist newspaper founded by Dorothy Day. All of his work exhibits great compassion for human suffering. A collection of some of his works was published in 1992 by Orbis Books under the title: *Fritz Eichenberg: Works of Mercy.*

    Fritz Eichenberg: A Portfolio of Prints (also available from Orbis Books) and suitable for framing, includes these etchings: "Christ in the Breadlines" (1953), "The Black Crucifixion" (1963), "The Lord's Supper" (1953), "Christ of the Homeless" (1982), "The Long Loneliness" (1952) and "The Peaceable Kingdom" (1950*)*. Any of these etchings could well serve as a focus point because they are visual meditations on the words of Christ. During this *Improving* Movement those in discernment are striving to improve each option under consideration until they become the very best that can be imagined within the yearning of God.

    For example, if your congregation is faced with possibilities for expanding the church's feeding of the hungry, you might ask the group to contemplate the etching "Christ in the Breadlines." These questions could be asked of the group: "What is to be said about the posture of the persons waiting to be fed?" "How is Jesus in relationship with each of the personified figures?" "What might the conversations, or the silences, be about?" "What does the color of the etching say to you?"

    Rory Cooney offers us a hymn most pertinent for the *Improving* Movement, "Jerusalem, My Destiny." I will quote the second verse and the chorus just to wet your appetite for the entire hymn:

"See, I leave the past behind; a new land calls to me.
Here among you now I find a glimpse of what might be.

Chorus:
I have fixed my eyes on your hills, Jerusalem, my destiny!
Though I cannot see the end for me, I cannot turn away.
We have set our hearts for the way; this journey is our
destiny.
Let no-one walk alone. The journey makes us one. "[68]

---

[68] Rory Cooney, <u>Jerusalem, My Destiny</u>, <u>Gather Comprehensive</u>, (Chicago, IL: GIA Publications, Inc., 1994).

As the group progresses during the *Improving* Movement, it is good to pause and ask: "What hopes are part of our spiritual discernment for the next few weeks or months?" Also: "What need do we have to revisit any of the other Movements?"

The activity of trying to "make art" requires a desire, a certain drive, a constant striving for something better, and some dissatisfaction. I continue to admire potters whom I've seen covered with clay, surrounded by partially finished pots needing to be trimmed or decorated, faced with hundreds of pounds of clay waiting to be wedged and thrown on the wheel, glazes to be mixed and kilns to be fired. They often work late into the night. The very nature of their art, its very essence, is practiced in the artists' physical movements toward aesthetic change and improvement of the vessel being created.

Clay is part of our connection with the earth. The *Improving* Movement might be a good time, individually or as a total group, to work with clay. Create a symbol for each path the group has been *Exploring*. During this Movement reshape the clay, add onto the symbol, or have sections removed from the symbols. In the end the clay will be changed. In a sense, each piece will be more than what it was in the beginning. So will each option. *"Like clay in the hands of the potter, so are you in my hands, O Israel" (Jeremiah 18:7).*

Water, along with earth, air and fire, has long been regarded as a major shaper of the earth, circulating in underground caverns and emerging as geysers and mountain springs and lakes. Water joins with other waters to become rivers and oceans, larger bodies than it could be on its own. It may be helpful during this *Improving* Movement to reflect on each option under consideration and visualize it as a particular path of water. Or, if you are outdoors by a stream, let that water become your symbol. Then consider this: "Are there streams (or elements) from the other paths (options) which would enhance this stream by joining it?"

When one scoops up just a handful of water, it seems that nothing could be weaker than that little bit of water. But when a large body of water rushes up against something hard or resistant to it, it may very well alter the landscape. Look closely to see how your landscape of options can yet be improved.

Each option under consideration could be mind-mapped on a distinct piece of newsprint or wallboard. Draw a circle, which will form the nucleus of a flower, a daisy, for example. In the center of the circle, write as succinctly as possible the option under consideration. Then

102

write ways to "better up" the option as petals on the flower. Do allow adequate time for silence between statements. After each statement is mind-mapped, it is good to affirm the improvements as a group, perhaps in song with a familiar "Alleluia" refrain. This action gives the group a sense of ownership for how each option now appears, and impetus to move into the *Weighing* Movement.

Chapter Five

Weaving Ritual & The Arts Throughout The Movements Of Weighing -- Closing -- Resting

The Movements of *Weighing, Closing* and *Resting* are captured under the heading *Harvesting the Yield* in spiritual discernment. These Movements also should not be considered in haste. Their strength is contingent upon the dialogue and prayer proceeding them and which will continue as essential elements throughout the content of these particular Movements.

We humans once believed that the earth was flat. But with continually evolving scientific theories and corresponding technology, we've come to see the earth as round. Scientists even keep delving into many new and surprising creations previously unknown to us!

Faithful, prayerful pursuit in a process of spiritual discernment is also capable of radically transforming the seemingly familiar and affecting new and energetic relationships. In the past, simplicity in a process of decision making usually meant eliminating "unnecessary" conversations, research, things, events, people, etc. In today's new paradigm of decision making, simplicity means striving toward oneness, bringing everything (all the wisdom, prayer, research, etc.) together into a balanced whole. Likewise, the old paradigm of decision making which emphasized order and clarity defined "chaos" as confusion. In the new paradigm, "chaos" means life is never the same because it keeps responding and growing from every experience. It is within the context of this new paradigm that we proceed in spiritual discernment.

HARVESTING THE YIELD
"A farmer harvests the yield. The good seeds which have been faithfully and patiently tended multiply and produce fruit which makes the hard work and waiting worthwhile. In discernment the leadings are weighed by testing for the same reason that wheat is harvested so that the good is

104

separated out. Then harvest closes with bagging the separated grain and finally rests with the bags safely placed in the storage barn."[69]

WEIGHING - Looking at all the options. Describe the tension between the options. Does there seem to be more integrity in one or more options? Are the options more or less important than previously thought during the *Exploring* Movement? Yes? No? Are they the same? Why, or why not?

Spiritual discernment involves sensing the movement of God's Spirit toward a particular option. It involves agreeing to look more in depth at a particular option, or to pray for a longer time over one or more of the options. It involves judging whether a particular option appears to be the best, most feasible, beneficial and Spirit-lead option.

There are many important questions to be asked of the discerners during this Movement: "Which option seems most impossible and why?" "What is thwarting your freedom to look intently at each option?" "Are you judging one option as counter productive, believing that no possible good can come of it?" "What is the prayer that you bring to God at this time?" Invite the sharing of personal prayers and affirm them with a spoken or sung response, e.g., "our hearts are restless until they rest in you."

In the situation mentioned earlier regarding the extensive piece of land and a former formation house for younger members in my religious congregation, it became apparent through periods of silence and dialogue that providing some land for open-space preservation meant a great deal to everyone involved. We gave this component of our eventual decision great integrity. This resonated with us because of our longstanding and deep commitment to all the land under our stewardship.

One way to facilitate members of the discerning group listening to each other well, is to have them briefly answer the simple question: "Why is this option important to you?" by beginning with the statement: "I believe...". Invite a few moments of silence in between responses. A

---

[69] Charles M. Olsen and Danny E. Morris. Discerning God's Will Together: A Spiritual Practice for the Church. Washington, D.C.: The Alban Institute; Nashville, TN: The Upper Room, 1997, p 70.

105

hymn refrain, or a refrain sung in rounds could also be used in between responses. A good resource, in addition to your own denominational hymnals, is *Songlines: Hymns, Songs, Rounds, Refrains for Prayer & Praise*, by Miriam Therese Winter.

The following is a Guided Imagery exercise suitable for use during the *Weighing* Movement. It was originally written for use for use on Epiphany, but feel free to use it, or a meditation of your own composition, as a springboard to engage discerners in prayerful reflection. The * is a cue for allowing silent time to engage deeper and deeper in the meditation.

Invite the participants to close their eyes and enter a quiet space deep within themselves. After three or four minutes lead them in meditation with these or similar words, allowing plenty of time after each statement or question:

> *Imagine that you hear a knock on the door of your quiet space.* *
> *When you open the door, you see the three Magi standing there.* *
> *What do they look like?* * *They tell you that they are going on a journey to find Jesus and they want you to join them. What places do you imagine them going to?* * *Will you join them? What do you tell them?* *
> *The Magi show you the gifts they have for the newborn Jesus.* *
> *Hold the gifts and carefully look at them.* * *You, too, say that you want to bring him a gift. What gift do you want to bring?* *
> *Since gifts are best when exchanged, what gift do you want to ask for during this time of discernment?* *
> *Go on the journey.* * *Give Jesus your gift.* * *What does he say and what does he do with it? How does this make you feel?* *
> *Now Jesus is giving you his gift in return. What is this gift?* *
> *What do you say to him? Speak to him from your heart.* *
> *When you are ready, come slowly back to this time and place.* *

This Guided Imagery may be followed by any extent of sharing that is acceptable to the group. Leading questions such as these may prove helpful: "Describe your relationship with the Magi on your mutual journey." "Describe the gift you brought to Jesus." "What gift did Jesus give you for this time of spiritual discernment?" "What new insight do you now own?" "If you could describe your experience of this meditation in a word or phrase, what would the word or phrase be?"

"What is it about one, or each option that might be seen as a gift?"

Since we are all human with varied emotions day in and day out, some participants may feel deeply touched and somehow changed by this experience of guided meditation. Others may remain untouched and somewhat removed from the action and the mystery. All discernmentarians can do is encourage persons to engage in their own personal resources of creative imagination and intuition.

God's Spirit can be slippery. *Weighing* in spiritual discernment isn't as easy as it might seem to be outside the context of a managerial culture. "Shepherd of My Heart", a hymn written by Francis Patrick O'Brien using the text of psalm 23, asks for guidance: "lead me home-ward through the dark into everlasting day."[70] Pausing to sing this hymn, or interspersing the singing of specific verses, or just the refrain during this *Weighing* Movement, will engulf your reflection in prayer. It will, as it were, replace the noise with tranquility. It will create an atmosphere in which interior peace becomes almost palpable.

Pictorial music might also assist discerners in *Weighing* the consonance and dissonance within options and among them. Listening to Franz Joseph Haydn's "Creation", published in 1810 and based on the book of Genesis, could provide fodder for the physical and spiritual energy needed within this Movement. Three angels sing the narrative, Gabriel (soprano), Uriel (tenor) and Raphael (bass), and the other two soloists are Adam (bass) and Eve (soprano). The oratorio is divided into three parts: Chaos and Days One through Four; Days Five and Six, and Adam and Eve. After each option for consideration has been named and before further dialogue ensues, listen to Chaos and Days One through Four.

The oratorio opens with Haydn's six minute orchestral depiction of chaos. While the music is bold and pushes limits, dissonance seem to gradually dissolve. The chaos is followed by a surprising "light." "The twenty-six measures preceding this chord set up the moment brilliantly: first Raphael (bass) sings, "In the beginning..." using the recitative style (with a wonderful depiction via a meandering line in the strings after the text, "and the earth was without form and void"). The entrance of the chorus "sotto voce" [muted voice] gently and beautifully portrays the spirit of God moving upon the face of the waters; this is accompanied

---

[70] Francis Patrick O'Brien, Shepherd of My Heart, in Gather Comprehensive, (Chicago: GIA Publications, 1994).

107

very simply in the strings and the entire passage is marked pianissimo [very soft]. The statements *"and God said"* together with *"let there be light"* are deftly followed by at least two beats of silence, so that the big moment which immediately follows is isolated for greater effect.[71]

Part One, through Day Four, concludes with the famous chorus: *"The heavens are telling the glory of God."*[72] It is this to which the group strives in the *Weighing* Movement: to sift through the chaos and uncertainty of each option and come to discern what is God's light on the matter.

The icon *Christ of the Desert* might be gazed upon during this Movement. Robert Lentz writes about this icon: "This icon celebrates the richness of Syriac Christianity. The Syriac inscriptions in the upper corners read "Jesus Christ," and at the bottom, "Christ of the Desert." The Syriac language has ties to the earth that are deep and rich. It is more inclusive than most European languages. The theological experience of Syriac Christians is different because they have encountered the Gospel in such a language. Theirs is an unhellenized expression—one that is neither Europeanized or westernized. ... A constant theme in Syriac literature is a homesickness for Paradise, a desire to restore Paradise on earth."[73]

"Which option appears to have more elements of "paradise" in it?" "Which path across the desert would Christ choose to walk?" "Which option is most faithful to your traditions?"

Another icon for consideration is *Jesus Breaking Bread* by John Giuliani, also available from Bridge Building Images. This icon is of a Navajo Christ sitting upright and breaking bread above a bowl of wine and a ceremonial basket. He wears a traditional Navajo velvet shirt, a cut-glass necklace and a third phrase chief blanket. Underneath and behind him are Navajo blankets of varying weavings.

"Which option seems in right relationship with your charism, or seems to best fill the ceremonial basket?" "Of the possible options (weavings), which clearly reveals the sacred to you?" "Which option seems to celebrate the spiritual vision of the followers of Christ?"

---

[71]Jonathan Saylor, "A Celebration of Haydn's Creation", Christianity And The Arts, May-July, 1997, p 24.

[72]Ibid.

[73] Robert Lentz. Christ of the Desert. Burlington, VT: Bridge Building Images, 1990.

A pertinent poem for this movement is Robert Frost's "A Road Less Traveled." This poem could be read, illustrated, choreographed for movement by the group, or mimed in a dimly lit space by one or more persons wearing white gloves.

Using the visual image of a spiral around a magnetic core of God's yearning, found on page sixty-eight of *Discerning God's Will Together: A Spiritual Practice for the Church*, discerners have come to view and experience spiritual discernment as a process in which the Movements build upon each other instead of being independent of each other. The cyclical pattern of discernment moves both inward and outward, changing course and momentum. There is inherent complexity and simplicity, chaos and holistic integration happening throughout the process. The attractor is God's Spirit within us, calling us to transformation and a deeper faith.

CLOSING – Closure is brought to the explorations by choosing the option given the most weight as Spirit-led. Discerners ask: Which option will most benefit God's people? Which option will nourish our souls? Which option will most fully continue the deeds of Jesus? What is our readiness and willingness to do what our choice requires? Is this choice coming from a loving place within myself/ourselves and not out of ego, selfishness or some other flawed place?

This Movement in spiritual discernment allows time for reflecting, musing, pondering, praying and mulling over the options. It calls for deep prayer that God's Spirit may direct us even in ways we can't predict. This Movement may, though not necessarily so, involve some bitter sweetness. It is a time for praying to God for true light, for seeing how the pieces of the puzzle fit together, perfectly, or not so perfectly.

Margaret Wheatley, in *Leadership and the New Science*, challenges her readers not to be afraid of creative energy in the universe. I believe her words apply to all seekers in spiritual discernment: "Perhaps if we understand the deep support we have from natural processes, it will help dispel some of the fear. It is not that we are moving toward disorder when we dissolve current structures and speak of worlds without boundaries. Rather, we are engaging in a fundamentally new relationship with order... The result is evolution, the organization of information into new forms. Life goes on, richer, more creative than before."[74] Discerners need to live with an evolutionary spirit, engaging in the present moment and moving into the new when they know that the right time has come.

The following sections of a prayer entitled "Meditation For A Theadbare Moment" by Mary Jo Leddy, might well set the tone for beginning this Movement:

"How do we discover the meaning of this moment?
Perhaps not how but where.
Where are the places, the spaces,
to position ourselves for the future?
Where should we place ourselves
so the future may present itself?

We must place ourselves together
in prayer, on the periphery,
on pilgrimage.

Placing ourselves together in prayer:
Visions find their first voice
at the deepest level of our lives
deeper than the conscious or
self-conscious levels of our lives.
In that space where
we are who we truly are
where we are of God,
with God and for God
where our lives are threaded with others
in a seamless garment of Spirit.

---

[74]Wheatley, Margaret. <u>Leadership and the New Science</u>. San Francisco, CA: Berrett Koehler Publishers, Inc., 1992, p 119.

In this space visions are born.
In the in-between of our prayer
beyond isolation,
beyond superficial togetherness
let us dwell in silence
together--to wait, to listen.
Let us nourish this prayer
with the symbols and stories of
our outrageous faith.
Let us read the Scriptures together
letting the words form
in the silence of our being
letting the words shape
the words we have to speak together.
Let us wait in the hope
of co-authoring a new chapter.
Let us hold ourselves
in readiness for a vision. [75]

In Native American cultures we find the circle image over and over again. We find it in the dances, in the art and in the shape of the lodgings. More than a symbol, the circle is the basis of American Indian beliefs: that everything is connected to everything else. All people, all of nature, and our Maker are all connected, always and forever. How can you creatively use a circle/circles to illustrate this *Closing* Movement? Large or small hulahoops could provide the frame, as could umbrella's, round placemats, baskets, vases, coins, etc. Invite the group members to mark them with words or illustrations that show the group's journey to this movement in spiritual discernment. Speak about the beliefs the group has come to own, and the new ways in which they are connected because of their prayerful time together.

The wonder of poetry might also strike a responsive chord in the discerners souls, assisting them to see their journey in faith in new

---

[75] Mary Jo Leddy, <u>Reweaving Religious Life Beyond The Liberal Model</u>. Mystic, CN: Twenty-Third Publications, 1990, pp. 169-170.

111

dimensions. Wendell Berry begins "Sabbaths: 1985 I" in this way:

> *"Not again in this flesh will I see*
> *the old trees stand here as they did,*
> *weighty creatures made of light, delight*
> *of their making straight in them and well,*
> *whatever blight or blindness was or*
> *made,*
> *however thought or act might fall.*
>
> *The burden of absence grows, and I pay*
> *daily the grief I owe to love*
> *for women and men, days and trees*
> *I will not know again. Pray*
> *for the world's light thus borne away.*
> *Pray for the little songs that wake and*
> *move.*[76]

Poems can enrich our spiritual lives, if we only will still ourselves long enough to linger over their words. Poetry that shares a theology of hope really does have divine power to transform and renew us.

I am reminded, while musing on this important Movement in spiritual discernment, of a book I perused recently entitled *Hunger of the Heart: Communion at the Wall*, by Larry Powell. The book pays tribute to the Vietnam Memorial in Washington D.C. as one of the greatest and saddest art works of this century. The cover is poignant. It is a black and white photo of one solitary person standing on a foggy night, midway along the length of the wall.

The discerners' experience of spiritual discernment may have led down some difficult, foggy, even wrenching paths, before clarity of vision could be reached. Whatever the path has been like, if it has been

---

[76]Impastato, David, ed., <u>Upholding Mystery: An Anthology of Contemporary Christian Poetry</u>, New York, NY: Oxford University Press, 1997, p 86.

true spiritual discernment, it has been a journey toward the light, and a journey that now needs to be reverenced and celebrated.

Participants in spiritual discernment who have gone through times of shadows, darkness and light, achieve genuine community and take pleasure, even delight in themselves as a collective. They know they have accomplished something together, discovered something of great value, and that they are onto something -- in this case, God's yearning for them.

Native Americans bless themselves and each other with sage smoke. Incense can be used in most settings, for both the aroma and the visual impact of smoke blessing the space and the people, as well as rising up to God in prayer. Or, a discernmentarian can use a beautiful candle with a lovely fragrance as a scent offering to God. It will contribute not only to the ambiance, but will remind the group that it is in Christ where true light and blessing is found.

The artful journey to this Movement in spiritual discernment has required the use of many tools: prayer, openness, knowledge, time, energy, etc. The group could choose to express their journey by naming the tools they've used and creating a collage that tells their story. The collage can be made out of any available material. A discernmentarian, during its creation, listens for themes running through the story and uses them to focus the group's concluding prayer.

Or, the group may be invited to create a mythical creature that expresses the group's long journey in spiritual discernment. Use everyone's vivid imaginations. The creature might be pencil sketched, created with yarn, string or basket weaving materials, or painted as a mural.

Another way of telling the story of the group's journey is to draw it on paper. When the drawing is completed, take a black pen and mark it into pieces of a puzzle. Cut the pieces apart, and at a subsequent gathering, the group could re-tell their story by re-assembling the puzzle.

One segment of a gathering of members of my religious congregation became entitled "Squabbles in the Tent." We were discussing serious issues that reflected differing ecclesiological viewpoints. (It was a healthy environment, and we're certainly still quite good friends.) But, our use of the tent imagery reminded me of Succot, or the Jewish Feast of Booths celebrated in the fall. It commemorates the dwelling in booths in the wilderness after the Exodus from Egypt (Leviticus 22:33-44) when Israel was summoned to remember God's protection and provision.

A succot is a simple frame structure that is freestanding or three-sided, using a wall of a house as a supporting structure. The roof is usually partially open to the sky, like a lattice, and the inside walls are decorated with pictures. To ritualize the *Closing* Movement in spiritual discernment, could you create such a space, perhaps under a trellis in warm weather, or could you construct such a miniature space using twigs or branches?

The group could prepare its own ritual for its succot. It might include eating fall fruits or vegetables, preparing a blessing over freshly baked bread that is then shared, followed by a benediction over the sacred space, where you have met. The benediction could be quite simple, such as: *"Spread over us your canopy of peace as we express thanks to you for your care of us."* In addition, some outreach to those less fortunate could be part of your thanksgiving.

The group may choose to close this Movement by praying together John 17, Jesus' prayer for oneness with all of creation. The prayer could be prayed in three sections: 1) the completion of Jesus' work; 2) the prayer for the disciples; and 3) the prayer for all believers. It may be prayed as the complete text by three distinct voices, or in more creative ways. One suggestion is to have the readers pause after particular verses for silence or for spontaneous prayers. Particular verses invite such prayer: "I am asking on their behalf; I am not asking on behalf of the world, but on behalf of those whom you gave me, because they are yours," (verse 9). You might ask the group: "On whose behalf do we seek God's mercy?" Then read: "I am not asking you to take them out of the world, but I ask you to protect them from the evil one," (verse 15), followed by this question: "What are our prayers as we prepare to close on our decision?" This prayer may conclude with a sharing of peace and/or a hymn such as "Now Thank We All Our God."

RESTING - Taking the test of the heart. Is there consolation or desolation in the decision? During this time, discerners pray for a growing resonance with God's Spirit:·

❖ a *knowing* that the decision arrived at is God's gift because the experience of each Movement centered upon God's yearning;

❖ a *feeling* deep in each heart that it rests well in the hollow of God's hand;

❖ an *action* that propels them forward into the deeper mystery that God's Spirit will yet do something marvelous with their decision.

There is great wisdom in the Biblical concept of Sabbath as a day of rest. Stepping into a period of *Resting* in spiritual discernment is absolutely essential if we are to experience our own richness of intuition, imagination and creativity. When we let the land of our heads and our hearts lie fallow for a period of time, we are able to put things in better perspective and come to a sense of inner truth, a sense of God's leading from within our souls.

God's yearning is our wellbeing. The deepest desire of God, the yearning of God, is my/our wellbeing. A serious spiritual discernment process removes distance between God and us. If the decision is what both God and I/we desire, there is harmony and peace. *Resting* in spiritual discernment is testing to determine if there is freedom from inordinate desires, uneasiness with the decision, and undue fear of its outcome. True *Resting* in the decision is that of achieving contemplation and centeredness in the Divine. It is living in a spirit of peace.

Desolation is the opposite. It is inconsolable, it is darkness, it is hopelessness regarding the decision and its outcome. It appears to be unhealthy for everyone, or some persons involved in it. It appears mechanical and lifeless, weak and not strong. It appears to be under pretexts of generosity or other virtues. It fosters confusion. It appears unbalanced and not of God. It disturbs the soul.

In the Rule of St. Ignatius, founder of the Jesuit Order, we find words to this effect: it is characteristic of the good spirit to stir up courage and strength, consolation, tears, inspirations and tranquility so that the persons may move forward in doing good. In Rules 1:3 and 4, Ignatius refers to the terms consolation and desolation. Consolation, or the peace of God, sustains one through times of spiritual dryness, when one feels no passion for much of life. It is then recognized as truly a gift when it appears in the smallest way or unexpected occasion. Ignatius describes consolation as every exercise in hope, faith and charity, and every interior joy. God is in it all. That's consolation. One's *Resting* in consolation involves one's knowing from where one is rooted and to where one is destined. As W. B. Yeats writes in his "A Prayer For Old Age": "God save us from the thoughts we think in the mind alone. Those who sing a lasting song sing in the marrow bone."[77]

Peace and tranquility have no edge, however, on *Resting*. God can also be experienced in weeping or bemoaning, a less culturally acknowledged form of consolation. When one is bemoaning a situation, one may see it very clearly. One may know that having made a decision, the action called for will be difficult to do, yet it really is God's yearning and needs to be done. Spiritual discernment is really not for spiritual wimps. There is a cost to following God's yearning.

There is an easily sung hymn, "I Say "Yes," Lord/Digo "Si," Senor", which could be intersperced throughout the conversation, silence and prayer of this Movement. At the conclusion of each verse sung by a cantor, the cantor sings "I say "Yes," my Lord" and the group repeats the words. The refrain is: "I say "Yes," my Lord, in all the good times, through all the bad times, I say "Yes," my Lord to every word you speak."[78] That fairly well sums up the stance we need to take in the *Resting* Movement.

In a 1987 sculptural work by George Segal, *Abraham's Farewell to Ishmael*, at the Sidney Janis Gallery in New York, both certainty and faith are suggested. Abraham embraces the son who was to be the future, Hagar faces the unknown of desert-exile, and Sarah watches in silence as one uncertain future is traded for another. The artist's work leads one to sense Abraham, Hagar, Ishmael and Sarah's conviction to face the uncertainty with conviction, and without panic. That inner conviction that all will be well comes through spiritual discernment. Faith is "the assurance of things hoped for, the conviction of things not seen" (Hebrews 11:1).

---

[77] Richard J. Finneran, ed. The Collected Poems of W. B. Yeats. New York, NY: Simon & Schuster, 1989, p 282.

[78] Donna Pena, I Say "Yes," Lord/Digo "Si," Senor, Gather Comprehensive, (Chicago, IL: GIA Publications, Inc., 1989).

116

A poem by Rose Marie Berger entitled "koinonia", gives us a flavor of what the *Resting* Movement is all about:

"pecan pickers and peace preachers
in southern georgia find tough nut of
gospel truth and wrap it for world in
sweet-as-honey chocolate for all to
taste
and see how good it can be

can't fight the power, only wait it out
invite it to dinner, nurse its children
when they lay low in fever
can't fight the power, only sit still
all night under vulnerable lamplight
and sing a little song to stay awake

better ones than you have fallen
asleep
in that vigil, but all is forgiven
and gentle arms surround as
children nestle down
some tossing with the fear of
unknown trucks
driving slow roads, while close beside
the other lays an unconscious arm
across
to protect and calm and wrap the
nightmare
in loving green hills and orchards
and the worn hands of many
grandparents
and others of strong shoulders, legs
and arms

come with me into the fields

*children of pecan pickers and peach
preachers
come and show me the glory
of this old land in southern georgia
where,
when the road is too weary,
god comes to rest"*[79]

It is in remembering the journey to the moment of *Resting* that
we are formed in faith for acting on what we've come to know as God's
yearning for us.

I have heard music described as "liquid light." Sacred music
serves to remind us that we have come from light and will return to the
light, which is God. We are, perhaps, drawn to "light" in spiritual
discernment like a moth is drawn to fire. Through times of cleansing,
listening, uncertainty, anger, and sometimes bliss, persons in spiritual
discernment need to be as roomy as liquid, and as supple as clay, letting
themselves experience the darkness, as well as light. Compline, or
evening prayer, a time for resting in God, begins with this spoken or
sung prayer: "Light and peace in Jesus Christ our Lord," and all
respond: "Thanks be to God." A beautiful arrangement for this
proclamation and the hymn "O Radiant Light" by Michael Joncas, is to
be found in *Praise God in Song*, an Ecumenical Daily Prayer, published
by GIA Publications.

In spiritual discernment, the *Resting* question is: "Do we know
in our hearts that this decision is of God, and is good?" Psalm 139
provides the prayer: "Search me, O God, and know my heart; test me
and know my anxious thoughts. See if there be any offensive way in me,
and lead me in the way everlasting."

Some available Taize music could help the group in spiritual
discernment dwell in the experience of God's presence, testing for God's
Spirit in the decision. Also, the hymn "I Heard the Voice of Jesus Say"
might further probe the inner voice, testing for consolation or desolation:
"I looked to Jesus, and I found in him my star, my sun, and in that light

---

[79] Rose Marie Berger, "koinonia," <u>Sojourners Magazine</u>, December, 1992, p 23.

118

of life I'll walk 'till traveling days are done."[80]

Here is a simple ritual you may choose to use during this Movement. In the center of the circle of those gathered, lay a long cord or a piece of thick yarn in a spiral array on the floor. Punctuate the array with random candles, placing one large candle in the middle of the circle. Invite the group to spend a few moments in silence thinking about a significant event or milestone in the life of the group's discernment. Break the silence by inviting one person to light a candle and share his/her reflection on the event. Follow this time by silence. Then, invite another person to do the same, and so on. Let the final candle (the large one in the middle) signify the present, where the group is now. The discernmentarian lights it and invites everyone to comment on the groups' present life with a short reflection or a prayer. This may be storytelling at its best, using a very simple but profound ritual.

In the *Resting* Movement, we are made aware that we are in the presence of something much bigger than a decision. If there is true consolation, we find ourselves embodying inner peace. And, we may even be surprised that the decision seems less expedient than usual decisions. In fact, it may be even somewhat prophetic. But the true test of consolation is that our hearts are at rest. Our hearts know that what has been discerned is God's yearning for us. If the decision is yet a difficult one to act upon, it is this very consolation that strengthens us to act upon it. We must trust, alongside Julian of Norwich, that "all shall be well and all shall be well and all manner of things shall be well."[81]

Ask the discerners: "Are you experiencing well-being, woe, or a mixture of both?" Invite them to test for their own peacefulness in the given time before your next gathering. As well, ask them to imagine how much peace they will have in the future because of their decision. "Are you able to connect your own yearning with God's yearning?" Invite them to picture the decision as ultimately going well, as it is in God's care.

There is wonderful folk art which discerners can turn to for reflection while *Resting* in their decision. An example of this is Edward Hicks' charming painting of The *Peaceable Kingdom*, circa 1834, which

---

[80] Ralph Vaughan Williams & Horatius Bonar, I Heard the Voice of Jesus Say, Gather Comprehensive, (Chicago, IL: GIA Publications, Inc., 1989).
[81] Julian of Norwich. Showings. trans. Edmund Colledge and James Walsh. New York, NY: Paulist Press, p 150.

is housed at the National Gallery of Art in Washington, DC. This painting, shown on page thirty-four of *Time* magazine's Spring, 1997 Special Issue, is his vision of harmony on earth, the Garden of Eden restored as in Isaiah 11:6: "The wolf also shall dwell with the lamb, and the leopard shall lie down with the kid...and a little child shall lead them." Some specific reflection questions based on this particular painting are: "How do we identify with this painting?" or "What grouping of animals/humans best symbolizes our spirit?" "As we conclude this time in discernment together, how might we continue to respond and grow from our common experience?"

Let's for a moment ponder the life of Mary, the mother of Jesus, a singular woman who transcends times and cultures, within this *Resting* Movement. Mary experienced many crucial moments during her life, but one in particular was the annunciation moment. Andrew Hudgins reflects on this moment as illustrated in his poem "The Cestello Annunciation" which is based on Sandro Botticelli's painting of the *Annunciation*:

> *"But her whole body pulls away.*
> *Only her head, already haloed, bows,*
> *acquiescing. And though she will, she's not yet said,*
> *Behold, I am the handmaid of the lord,*
> *a Botticelli, in his great pity,*
> *lets her refuse, accept, refuse, and think again."*[82]

The story told by Luke is of Mary's love-laden response to divine disclosure, to God's invitation after "she was greatly troubled..." by it (Luke 1:29). She eventually rested on God's word alone, not knowing all that it implied, only that it was God who issued the invitation. Then, full of wonder at the way in which God was dealing with her, she broke into this hymn of praise: "My soul glorifies the Lord, and my spirit rejoices in God my Savior..." (Luke 1:47-55).

Resting in spiritual discernment might well follow times of struggle and doubt. This is normal. But *Resting* should also follow active receptivity to God's yearning within us. When we experience this

[82] Impastato, David, ed, <u>Upholding Mystery: An Anthology of Contemporary Christian Poetry</u>. New York, NY: Oxford University Press, 1997, p 75.

oneness with God, we celebrate and offer praise. Hildegard of Bingen, a German mystic (1098-1179) renowned as a theologian, physician and composer wrote:

> *"Be not lax in celebrating,*
> *Be not lazy in the festive service of God.*
> *Be ablaze with enthusiasm.*
> *Let us be an alive, burning offering before*
> *the altar of God."[83]*

The Seattle Art Museum is home to a wonderful teak sculpture, *Obos 1*, by George Tsutakawa. It is made from the wood of a two hundred-year-old English schooner that was dismantled in Seattle in the mid-Twentieth Century. Tsutakawa's sculpture was inspired by an ancient act of thanksgiving. "Obos" is a Tibetan word for the ritually placed piles of rocks left by passersby at auspicious sites in the Himalayan Mountains. These cairns are built at mountain passes in thanksgiving for safe passage and at sites such as water sources, where the spiritual energy of the earth is believed to be potently expressed. As a sculptural form, Tsutakawa's *Obos 1* is concerned with balance and the relationship of solid form to space. "...it uses a totemic configuration to invoke a message of universality. Tsutakawa, born in Seattle and educated in Japan and the United States, intends that the sculpture express spiritual as well as physical balance, a harmony of form and content that surpasses specific cultural references."[84]

In the consolation we seek within the *Resting* Movement, we should possess gratitude to God and enthusiasm and passion for the future of our decision. An excerpt from a text written by Barbara Kunz Loots entitled "Great Is The Wonder" and based on John 4:35, provides a poetic prayer for *Resting* and then moving on. It could be recited during the construction of a rock, stick, clay form or brick cairn:

> *Fill us, O Lord, with spirit-given peace,*

---

[83] Uhlein, Gabriele, Meditation with Hildegard of Bingen, Santa Fe, NM: Bear and Company, 1993, p 126.

[84] Seattle Art Museum, Seattle, WA: The Seattle Art Museum, 1991, p 109.

Let grace abound, life-giving hope increase,
Show us the Christ in every human face,
Fashioned by love in every form and race.

Lead us beyond the narrow paths we know
Into the fields where ripened harvests grow,
Teach us to bring the healing word and deed
From your abundance to a world in need."[85]

Perhaps a discerner has composed a poem he or she wishes to share with the group as closure is near. That could well be a precious gift to the group. I treasure this poem by Dave Bielefeld, a former colleague of mine. It is entitled "The Fog":

"The Fog,
Playing at the window,
Covers the forest.
One lone tree,
Ignoring the shroud,
Survives the flood.

Like a player
Caught on the apron
When the curtain falls.

Before,
It was just
Part of the forest.

Now,
It stands alone
In clear view.

---

[85]Barbara K. Loots. Great Is The Wonder, Kansas City, MO: Hope Publishing Company, 1993.

Strange
How a veil
Both reveals and conceals. [86]

     May you have given this resting movement adequate time, enough time so that the decision will indeed rest well within you, and rest well in God.

---

[86] R. Dave Bielefeld. <u>Montana Priest</u>. Unpublished poems. 1988, p 33.

EPILOGUE

The use of ritual and the arts in spiritual discernment strengthens the connections or the threads that tie our present day living to the age-old story of our Christian heritage. In spiritual discernment these stories are woven more closely into a single thread, or one story, leading us into deeper spiritual insight.

In spiritual discernment we allow ourselves to be individually transformed. We are also privileged to take part in the personal transformation of others. Together we become the *Unfinished Symphony*. We become the clay pot in need of continual refining. We become the stained glass window reflecting colors which deepen with each encounter. We become the poem whose verses demand more-or-less rhythm or cadence.

Spiritual discernment is all about making decisions that cause us to move ever deeper into the life of God's Spirit. If we persevere in this spiritual practice over a lifetime we engage ourselves in the art-full practice of centering our lives in the Spirit of God. Ah, to partake of this richness! Let us continue on the journey.

GLOSSARY OF TERMS

Biblical/Theological Reflection: The practice of distilling wisdom from a Scripture story or passage and weaving it together with the story of an individual or a group, thereby giving insight into the ways of God's Spirit.

Centering Prayer: Prayer centered on the God within; a suspension of consciousness; a resting in God beyond thinking, image and emotions.

Charism: A gift of the Holy Spirit given to individuals or groups for the good of the community. The unique gift (1Cor 12:4-11) carries with it the responsibility of exercising it to renew the world.

Congregation: A community of believers who gather for common worship.

Corporate Spirituality: A faith community's practice of surrendering to God, ministering in the name of God, and naming God's presence.

Decision-making: The product of a process for seeking the wisdom of God in an open and inclusive way. One or more methods may be used, e.g., spiritual discernment.

Diocese: A Catholic or Episcopal community, usually circumscribed territorially, entrusted to the pastoral care of a Bishop.

Discernmentarian: A spiritual guide/director for an individual or a small or large group. This person helps the group know where they are in a spiritual discernment process, keeps the process moving, and keeps the focus on seeking the mind of Christ in a given matter.

Faith Community: A formal organization of persons with common beliefs and commitments, usually with designated leaders.

Guided Imagery: An imaginative meditation that serves to lead into a visual image, not necessarily one that is clear or precise.

Haiku: An unrhymed Japanese lyric poem having a fixed three-line form containing five, seven and five syllables respectively; a form that require no meter or rhyming.

Icon: A likeness or image gazed upon in contemplation for the purpose of offering access into the invisible..

Iconographer: A person who writes/paints an icon.

Iconography: A pictoral representation of a specific subject, usually a person.

Laybryinth: A winding path for prayerful walking; a common symbol in the cathedral churches of Europe in the Middle Ages.

Lectio Divina: A process of engaging oneself with a Scripture passage; that involves prayerful reading, meditation, prayer and contemplation.

Liturgist: A person who leads a group in spiritual practices/worship.

Liturgy of the Hours: A daily rhythm of personal and communal prayer. Each hour has particular themes, prayers and hymns.

Mantra: A sacred word or phrase one keeps repeating in order to move into interior silence.

Movements in Spiritual Discernment: The ten dynamics that constitute a process of spiritual discernment, i.e., Framing, Grounding, Shedding, Rooting, Listening, Exploring, Improving, Weighing, Closing, Resting.

Ritual: The form, method or order of engaging in religious ceremony.

Sage: An experienced person of faith to whom members of a religious community look for spiritual wisdom.

Spiritual Discernment: A spiritual practice in which one sees to the heart of the matter, or as best can be determined, from God's perspective. A prayerful process calling for humility and patient listening to many sources of experience and wisdom.

Spirituality: A life of finding one's center in God and leading from that center as the indwelling Spirit of God prompts.

Story-telling: The personal or communal sharing of an account of human experience. This ancient practice forms identity, establishes and re-creates communities, and generates passion for life when it is practiced.

Symbol: A material object or art piece representing something abstract, e.g., a quality, a relationship.

BIBLIOGRAPHY

BOOKS

Bonhoeffer, Deitrich. Life Together. New York, NY: Harper and Row, 1954.

Bovini, Guiseppe. Ravenna Mosaics. Greenwich, CN: New York Graphic Society, 1956.

Briffa, Salvino. That I May See: A Prayerful Discovery through Imagination. Salem, OR: Dominion Books, 1986.

Brueggemann, Walter. Gathering the Church in the Spirit, Reflections on Exile and the Inscrutable Wind of God. Decatur, GA: CTS Press, 1995.

Carmelite Monastery. Liturgy of the Hours. Indianapolis, IN: Carmelite Monastery, 1992.

Catholic Bishops of Appalachia. This Land is Home to Me. Webster Springs, WV: Catholic Committee on Appalachia, 1990.

Chittister, Joan. A Passion for Life: Fragments of the Face of God. Maryknoll, NY: Orbis Books, 1996.

Dierks, Leslie. Making Mosaics: Designs, Techniques and Projects. New York, NY: Sterling Publishing Company, 1974.

Dillard, Annie. Pilgrim at Tinker Creek. New York: Harper & Row Publishers, 1974.

Dillard, Annie. Teaching A Stone To Talk. New York: Harper & Row Publishers, 1982.

Eichenberg, Fritz. Fritz Eichenberg: A Portfolio of Prints. Maryknoll, NY: Orbis Books, 1995.

Eichenberg, Fritz. Fritz Eichenberg: Works of Mercy. Maryknoll, NY: Orbis Books, 1992.

Eliot, T. S. Ash Wednesday. New York, NY: Harcourt Brace & Co., 1934.

Elliot, Marion. Paper Making. New York, NY: Henry Holt & Co., 1994.

Esquivel, Julia. Threatened With Resurrection. Elgin, IL: Brethren Press, 1982.

Finneran, Richard J. The Collected Poems of W. B. Yeats. New York, NY: Simon & Schuster, Inc., 1989.

Foley, Edward. _From Age To Age_. Chicago, IL: Liturgy Training Publications, 1991.

Forest, Jim. _Praying With Icons_. Maryknoll, NY: Orbis Books, 1997.

Fry, Christopher. _A Sleep of Prisoners_. New York, NY: Oxford University Press, 1951.

Gardner, Helen, ed. _Oxford Book of English Mystical Verse._ London: Oxford University Press, 1972.

Gerstein, Marc and Lynette Wrigley. _Stained Glass, Contemporary Crafts_. New York, NY: Henry Holt & Co., 1995.

Granger, Christine. _Mary, Mother of My Lord_. Toronto, CAN: Novalis, 1997.

Hall, Thelma. _Too Deep For Words. Rediscovering Lectio Divina_. Mahwah, NJ: Paulist Press, 1988.

Harris, Maria. _Proclaim Jubilee, A Spirituality for the Twenty-first Century_. Louisville, KY: Westminster John Knox Press, 1996.

Head, Rhoda, et al. ed. _Well of Living Waters_. Los Angeles, CA: C. G. Jung Institute, 1977.

Hiller, Julio and Nancy G. Heller, eds. _North American Women Artists of the 20th Century, a Biographical Dictionary_. New York & London: Garland Publishing, Inc., 1995.

Holmes, Oliver Wendell. _The Aristocrat of the Breakfast Table_. 1891.

Huck, Gabe. _How Can I Keep From Singing?_ Chicago, IL: Liturgy Training Publications, 1989.

Impastato, David, ed. _Upholding Mystery: An Anthology of Contemporary Christian Poetry_. New York, NY: Oxford University Press, 1997.

Johnson, Luke Timothy. _Scripture & Discernment, Decision Making In The Church_. Nashville, TN: Abingdon Press, 1983.

Julian of Norwich. _Showings_. trans. Edmund Colledge and James Walsh. New York, NY: Paulist Press, 1978.

Keyte, Hugh and Andrew Parrott, eds. _The New Oxford Book of Carols_. New York, NY: Oxford University Press, 1972.

Lauppi, Walter. _Mosaics with Natural Stones_. Translated by Manly Banister. New York, NY: Sterling Publishing Company, 1974.

Lazarev, Viktor N. _The Russian Icon From Its Origins to the Sixteenth Century_. Collegeville, MN: The Liturgical Press, 1997.

Leddy, Mary Jo. _Reweaving Religious Life Beyond The Liberal Model_. Mystic, CN: Twenty-Third Publications, 1990.

Mass, Robin and Gabriel O'Donnell, eds. Spiritual Traditions for the Contemporary Church. Nashville, TN: Abingdon Press, 1990.
McDade, Carolyn. Sister, Carry On. Wellfleet, MA: Carolyn McDade and Friends, 1992.
McKinney, Mary Benet. Sharing Wisdom. Allen, TX: Tabor Publishing, 1983.
McManus, John and Eugene d'Aquili, Charles Louhlin, Tom Burns, eds. The Spectrum of Ritual: A Biogenetic Structural Anslysis. New York, NY: Columbia University Press, 1979.
McNamee, John P., Robert F. McGovern. Clay Vessels and Other Poems. Kansas City, MO: Sheed & Ward, 1995.
Menzel, Peter and Faith D'Aluisio. Women in the Material World. Santa Fe, NM: Sierra Club Books, 1996.
Metzger, Bruce M. and Roland E. Murphy, eds. The New Oxford Annotated Bible. New York, NY: Oxford University Press, 1991.
Morneau, Robert F. Mantras from a Poet: Jessica Powers. Kansas City, MO: Sheed & Ward, 1992.
Morseth, Ellen. Call to Leadership: Transforming the Local Church. Kansas City, MO: Sheed & Ward, 1993.
Morseth, Ellen. New Board/Council Member Orientation. Kansas City, MO: Worshipful-Work: Center for Transforming Religious Leadership, 1996.
Nouwen, Henri. Behold The Beauty Of The Lord: Praying With Icons. Notre Dame, IN: Ave Maria Press, 1987.
Olsen, Charles M. Transforming Church Boards into Communities of Spiritual Leaders. Washington, D.C.: The Alban Institute, 1995.
Olsen, Charles M. and Danny E. Morris. Discerning God's Will Together: A Spiritual Practice for the Church. Washington, DC: The Alban Institute; Nashville, TN: The Upper Room, 1997.
Powell, Larry. David Lebelle and Cara Sutherland. Hunger of the Heart: Communion at the Wall. Dubuque, IA: Islewest Publishing, 1995.
Roberts, Elizabeth and Elias Amidon, eds. Earth Prayers from around the World: 365 Prayers, Poems and Invocations for Honoring the Earth. San Francisco, CA: Harper Collins, 1991.
Rosenblum, Naomi, Walton Rowle, Ed. A World History of Photography. New York, NY: Abbeville Press, Inc., 1984.
Rupp, Joyce. Fresh Bread and Other Gifts of Spiritual Nourishment. Notre Dame, IN: Ave Maria Press, 1988.

Scotto, Dominic F. The Liturgy of the Hours. Petersham, MA: St. Bede's Publications, 1987.

Seattle Art Museum, Seattle, WA: The Seattle Art Museum, 1991.

Sexton, Ann. The Awful Towing Toward God. Boston, MA: Houghton Mifflin Co., 1975.

Siegfried, Regina and Robert Morneau, eds. Selected Poetry of Jessica Powers. Kansas City, MO: Sheed & Ward, 1989.

Sisters of Charity, BVM. Constitutions. Dubuque, IA: Sisters of Charity, BVM, 1989.

Simcoe, Mary Ann, ed. The Liturgy Documents. Chicago, IL: Liturgy Training Publications, 1978.

Tansey, Richard G. and Fred S. Kleiner. Gardner's Art Through the Ages. Fort Worth, TX: Harcourt Brace College Publishers, 1996.

Teresa of Avila. The Interior Castle. Translated by Kieran Kavanaugh & Otilio Rodriguez. New York, NY: I.C.S. Publications, 1980.

Tuyen, P.D. Classic Origami. New York, NY: Sterling Publishing Company, 1995.

Uhlein, Gabriele. Meditation with Hildegard of Bingen. Santa Fe, NM: Bear and Company, 1993.

Von Goethe, Johann Wolfgang. Wilhelm Meister's Apprenticeship. Book 5, 1786-1830.

Wheatley, Margaret J. Leadership and the New Science. San Francisco, CA: Berrett-Koehler Publishers, Inc., 1994.

White, James F. Introduction To Christian Worship. Nashville, TN: Abingdon Press, 1992.

Williamson, Marianne. A Return to Love. New York, NY: Harpercollins, 1992.

Winter, Miriam Therese. Songlines: Hymns, Songs, Rounds, Refrains for Prayer & Praise. New York: NY, Crossroad Publishing Co., 1996.

HYMNALS

<u>Gather Comprehensive</u>, Chicago, IL: GIA Publications, Inc., 1994.
<u>Music Issue 1997</u>, Portland, OR: Oregon Catholic Press, 1997.
<u>Praise God in Song, Ecumenical Daily Prayer</u>, Chicago, IL: G.I.A. ·
Publications, Inc., 1979.
<u>Presbyterian Hymnal, Hymns, Psalms, and Spiritual Songs</u>, Louisville,
KY: Westminster/John Knox Press, 1990.
<u>The United Methodist Hymnal</u>, Nashville, TN: The United Methodist
Publishing House, 1989.

AUDIO TAPES

Jacques Berthier, "Jesus, Remember Me," <u>Jubilate</u>. Chicago, IL: G.I.A.
Publications, Inc., 1991.
Jacques Berthier, "Our Darkness/La Tenebre," <u>Resurrexit</u>. Chicago, IL:
G.I.A. Publications, Inc., 1991.
Jacques Berthier, "Nada Te Turbe," <u>Resurrexit</u>. Chicago, IL: G.I.A.
Publications, Inc. 1984.
Jacques Berthier, "Veni Sancte Spiritus," <u>Taize - Cantate!</u> Chicago, IL:
G.I.A. Publications, 1981.
Bruce Kurnow, <u>Earth Rhythms</u>. Canada: NorthWord Press, Inc, 1993.
Johann Pachelbel, "Pachabel Canon in D Major," <u>The Pachelbel Canon
and Other Baroque Favourites in Digital Sound</u>. New York, NY: The
Moss Music Group, Inc., 1981.
Mike Rowland, <u>The Fairy Ring</u>. Milwaukee, WI: Music Design, Inc.,
1982.
Antonio Vivaldi, <u>The Four Seasons</u>. Holland: The Decca Record
Company LTD, 1970.
Danny Wright, <u>Shadows</u>. Arlington, TX: Moulin D'OR Recordings.

VIDEO TAPES

Berrett-Koehler Publishers, Inc., <u>Leadership and the New Science</u>. San
Francisco, CA, 1994.
Kino International Corp., <u>Daughters of the Dust</u>. New York, NY.
Orien Pictures Corp., <u>Babette's Feast</u>. Los Angeles, CA: Franciscan
Communications, 1989.